For over twenty years, Gavin McCrone was Chief Economic Adviser to successive Secretaries of State for Scotland and head of two Scottish Government Departments in what was then the Scottish Office: the Industry Department for Scotland and the Scottish Development Department.

Prior to his time in government, he lectured in economics at Glasgow and Oxford Universities and in the 1990s he returned to his earlier career first as a professor at Glasgow University and then at the Edinburgh University Business School. He has written and lectured about the Scottish economy over a period of many years and in 1996 he undertook a study on European Monetary Union and Regional Development for the Bank of Scotland.

He is a Fellow of the Royal Society of Edinburgh and served as the Society's Vice President from 2002 to 2005. In 2003 he was Vice-Chairman of the Society's Inquiry into the Crisis in the Scottish Fishing Industry and in 2007–08 Chairman of their Inquiry into the Future of Scotland's Hill and Island Areas.

AFTER BREXIT

THE ECONOMICS OF
SCOTTISH INDEPENDENCE

GAVIN McCRONE

BIRLINN

First published in 2022 by
Birlinn Limited
West Newington House
10 Newington Road
Edinburgh
EH9 1QS

www.birlinn.co.uk

2

ISBN: 978 1 78027 762 2

British Library Cataloguing-in-Publication Data

A catalogue record for this book is available from the British Library
Papers used by Birlinn are from well-managed forests and
other responsible sources

Typeset by Initial Typesetting Services, Edinburgh
Printed and bound by Clays Ltd, Elcograf S.p.A.

*For my family, friends and all those concerned
for the future of Scotland*

Contents

Preface

Eight years ago, I published *Scottish Independence: Weighing Up the Economics*. My book ran to two editions, the second being a much-expanded version of the first, and both sold out before the 2014 Scottish referendum. The book was intended to be a non-partisan explanation for the general reader of the issues that Scottish independence would involve. Much that I wrote then is still relevant but that was before Brexit took the UK out of the EU, with Scotland voting by over 60 per cent to stay in. I had not intended to revise or update my 2014 book. But Brexit has changed the issue in fundamental respects and twenty of the polls over the last two years have now shown a majority in favour of independence. The latest indications are that those in favour and those against are now more finely balanced and that support for independence may have slightly declined, although still very strong. Polling results, however, are volatile and may be affected both by unexpected events and by the campaigning of the political parties. The issue therefore remains of major importance for Scotland and, in view of the continuing strength of opinion both for and against independence, I felt that the issue had to be revisited. If there is another Scottish referendum, there must be many who will wonder how the case for and against independence has changed. I have therefore written this short book setting out how I believe the case now stands. I make no secret of my views on Brexit, which I believe to be seriously damaging to Scotland and its economy, but I have tried, as in the earlier book, to set out the issues on independence in a fair and non-partisan way. I have never been a member of a political party but, for very many years, have taken a close interest in the Scottish economy and policies intended to improve the wellbeing of the Scottish people. Those who read this book will draw their own conclusions both for and against independence from what I have written. That is how I would wish it to be, as there is much to be aware of before voting in a second referendum, if such a referendum takes place. If this book helps the reader to be better informed before such a vote and much better informed than the United Kingdom's electorate was before the 2016 EU referendum, that is my aim.

The bulk of this book was written in the early months of 2021 but, while it was with the publishers, before it actually went to press, I was able to take account of the latest figures on Scotland's finances in 'Government Expenditure and Revenue Scotland 2020–21' (GERS), published in August 2021. This enabled many of the statistics to be updated.

In writing the book, I have been greatly helped by my son, Angus, and by Peter Mackay, a former colleague, both of whom kindly read the whole text and made many helpful suggestions and editorial improvements. I have had helpful comments from Jeremy Peat, also a former colleague and a former chief economist at the Royal Bank of Scotland, from Sir David Edward, a former British judge at the European Court of Justice, and Christophe Hillion, professor of European law at Oslo, Leiden and Gothenburg. I am especially grateful to my wife who has tolerated, without complaint, the time I have spent writing. But the responsibility for what I have written and the opinions expressed are entirely my own.

Gavin McCrone

Introduction

There are probably many in the rest of the United Kingdom who wonder how it has come about that there is pressure in Scotland for another independence referendum and why, after over 300 years of union, there are apparently many people who want to re-establish Scotland once again as an independent state. Despite the long period of union and its success in many respects, the people of Scotland have never lost their consciousness of a separate identity. Indeed, that sense seems to have become stronger during my lifetime. Maybe the forces that made the union a success have become less strong. Although, in the eighteenth and nineteenth centuries, the Jacobite rebellions and, in the Highlands, the clearances and potato famine all gave rise to discontent and difficulty, there were many successes and things to be proud of – the age of enlightenment in which Scotland played such a major part, the economic development in which Scotland was at the forefront of innovation and the increasing prosperity of the country. There was also the crucial role of the Scottish regiments, first in the Napoleonic Wars and then in the two world wars, together with the major part Scotland has played internationally. Unlike Ireland, Scotland never suffered serious misgovernment. The Act of Union enabled Scotland to trade with the English colonies of the time, especially in North America, to keep its own legal system, its educational system and, most importantly at the time, its own Presbyterian Kirk in contrast to the Anglican Church in England.

In the twentieth century, a much stronger sense has developed of the responsibility of government for people's welfare. Instead of just accepting the inevitability of things that happened, there was a much greater awareness of how they might be changed, hopefully for the better. And so, when the economy on which Scotland had depended for so long was forced to change, this was no longer seen as inevitable but something that government had a responsibility to manage. Scotland's very success in the nineteenth-century economy began to become a problem in the twentieth as the older heavy industries on which Scotland's prosperity had depended began to decline.

Scotland suffered very serious unemployment in the interwar period and, although the heavy industries recovered during the war – a recovery which lasted throughout the 1940s and early 1950s – there then began a long period of decline. Shipbuilding, steel, heavy engineering, textiles and coal mining had all been of major importance to the Scottish economy and all began to lose their role as the source of the economy's growth and prosperity. Unemployment, though relatively low compared with pre-war and also by some later standards, was generally twice the UK average and emigration both to the rest of the UK and overseas was a major factor, the rate in the 1960s being particularly high.

These problems were not unique to Scotland. The north of England, Merseyside and South Wales suffered the same problems and UK governments had tried to tackle them with regional policy measures that were designed to attract jobs and investment to the areas that suffered unemployment and industrial decline. While these measures did not completely cure the problem, they did have considerable success but this was not always sufficiently recognised. Perhaps Scotland's sense of a separate identity and the existence of the Scottish

National Party (SNP) gave the problem a particular focus that did not exist in the north of England.

The SNP had been established as a political party between the two world wars. For many years, it attracted little political support, although it gained a seat in the UK Parliament in a by-election in 1945, only to lose it a few months later in the general election.[1] The party only began to become a significant force in 1968 when Winnie Ewing won the Hamilton by-election, which was followed by a substantial success in the Scottish local government elections. Edward Heath, as leader of the opposition, then made the first commitment to parliamentary devolution in a speech at Perth in 1968. In the 1970 general election, the SNP won only one seat, the Western Isles, in the UK Parliament, although Margo MacDonald won Govan for them soon afterwards, in a by-election in 1973. This, however, was the time when major oil discoveries were made in the North Sea, in what would have been Scottish waters had it been an independent state. This appeared, at least for a considerable time, to put an end to any credibility in the argument frequently peddled by UK politicians that Scotland would be worse off if it was independent. The SNP won seven seats in the spring 1974 general election and eleven in the election later that year.

It was in response to this that the first proposals for parliamentary devolution were developed by the UK Labour government and these were the subject of the first referendum in 1979. Although a majority of those voting were in favour of the proposals, they were less than 40 per cent of the total electorate, a condition that had been inserted by an amendment in the Bill. So devolution was not enacted at that time. There followed the election of a Conservative government led by Mrs Thatcher, who had no intention to legislate for devolution. The 1980s were a very difficult time in Scotland, as they also were in the north of England. A huge amount of manufacturing industry disappeared with resulting high unemployment rates and regional policy was greatly weakened, as it did not accord with the government's economic philosophy. There was considerable success, however, in attracting foreign investment to Scotland, especially in the electronics industry. This was mainly from the United States but also from Japan. Unfortunately, this was not to last with many companies leaving again in the 1990s to take advantage of cheaper labour elsewhere.

During the 1980s and early 1990s, the Labour Party held a large majority of the Scottish seats in the UK Parliament which coincided with the loss of so much of manufacturing industry. The party remained committed to devolution but to no avail with a large Conservative majority in the UK Parliament. This led, in my view, to a feeling of frustration and what amounted to something similar to disenfranchisement of the Scottish electorate. What was the use of repeatedly voting for a party that never gained a majority because of votes cast elsewhere in the UK? The Labour Party had won 50 seats out of Scotland's 72 but was largely powerless. Following the 1987 general election, therefore, the Campaign for a Scottish Assembly established a Constitutional Steering Committee. Chaired by Sir Robert Grieve, it included a group of distinguished Scots who urged the creation of a Scottish Constitutional Convention to draw up a scheme for a Scottish Assembly. This became known as a Claim of Right and it harked back to an Act of the Scottish Parliament in 1689, when Presbyterian Scotland found that King James VII was imposing elements of his Catholic religion on the country. The new Claim was supported by the Labour Party, the Liberal Democrats and many distinguished Scots. It led in due course, when once again there was a Labour government, to the 1997 devolution referendum, which by a large majority endorsed the proposal to set up a Scottish Parliament and to give it tax-raising powers.

In November 2020, Boris Johnson was quoted as saying that devolution was a mistake, presumably because it enabled the SNP to form a government. But, in the early years, of course, it was a Labour–Liberal Democrat coalition that formed the Scottish government. Such was the pressure for devolution after the Thatcher years, that, had the Labour Party not honoured its pledge, all that would have happened would have been a massive majority of Scottish seats for the SNP in the next UK election, followed by a constitutional crisis. The SNP gained the largest number of seats in the 2007 Scottish election and formed a minority government. This was followed by an overall majority in 2011, something that was thought impossible for any party to achieve with the system of proportional representation that was adopted for the Parliament. It led to a demand for a referendum on independence, which David Cameron, then UK Prime Minister in a coalition government, agreed to for 2014. In the event, that referendum delivered a majority for the status quo but the result was closer than many had originally expected and, at one stage in the period immediately before the vote, it looked as if those arguing for independence might just win.

Since then, there has been Brexit which the majority of Scots in every local authority area voted against and which is predicted by leading economic analysts to do serious damage to the Scottish economy. This book discusses the damage that Brexit is likely to do to Scotland – how it will affect trade with our main overseas market and investment from international companies and end support from the EU structural funds and the Erasmus scheme for students. It is already influencing the number of skilled foreign workers in the NHS, in care homes, in the hospitality industry and elsewhere who have come from Europe. On the other hand, if an independent Scotland sought to renew its links with the EU, that would require a customs border between Scotland and the rest of the UK. And leaving the UK single market would threaten the 60 per cent or so of Scottish trade with the rest of the UK, unless a satisfactory arrangement can be negotiated to reduce the impact of a hard EU border between Scotland and the rest of the UK. The implications of joining the EU as a full member compared with membership of the European

Free Trade Association (EFTA) and the European Economic Area (EEA) are therefore explained with the latter likely to be easier to negotiate and also less damaging.

There are likely to be substantial pressures on the budget of an independent Scotland, not just resulting from the need to balance the budget after independence but also pressing demands for more to be spent on education, health and social security. There would be a need for a greatly strengthened economic policy to improve the country's economic prospects and performance, so that these things can be afforded.

The days when the two main UK political parties had the bulk of the Parliamentary seats in Scotland between them have now gone. In those years, if the predominant political party in Scotland was not also the party of government, at least it was the main party of opposition which would have a chance of forming the next government. That is no longer the case and, just as majority votes for the Labour Party achieved nothing for Scottish voters in the Thatcher years, so votes for the SNP have very little effect on a Brexiteer Conservative government now. It is against this background that the campaign for a second Scottish referendum has to be seen.

The chapters that follow deal with the case for a referendum, what kind of referendum that should be and what the options for an independent Scotland might be, including: how it should relate to the EU and the rest of the UK (Chapters 1 and 2); the financial issues – budget deficit, debt, the balance of foreign payments and options for the currency (Chapter 3); other financial pressures – health, education, social care and welfare (Chapter 4); problems with managing the economy (Chapter 5); North Sea oil and future energy supplies (Chapters 6 and 7); the financial sector, mortgages and pensions (Chapters 8 and 9); and the European Union (Chapter 10). The last chapter provides a summary and conclusion.

Another referendum? If so, what kind?

At the time of the 2014 referendum on Scottish independence, SNP leaders said that it would be a once in a generation event. But, although the result of the referendum was 45 per cent for independence and 55 per cent for remaining in the United Kingdom, the issue has not gone away. Indeed, campaigning for independence has continued and there have been repeated demands for a second referendum. There can be no doubt that referenda are very divisive, splitting families and sometimes destroying friendships. The 2014 referendum in Scotland passed off peacefully but not without some unpleasantness. The EU referendum was the same. Another Scottish referendum would be equally divisive, if not more so. So would it be right to hold one?

Under the terms of the Scotland Act 1998, constitutional matters are reserved to the UK Parliament. The 2014 referendum took place with the agreement of the government of the UK, then led by David Cameron, probably in the expectation that it would resolve the matter once and for all. That might have been the case if the result had been a large majority for the status quo. But that turned out to be a spectacular misjudgement – indeed, shortly before the actual date, one of the polls had given a majority for independence, leading to last-minute promises of greater devolution, which have since been implemented.

None of this has satisfied those who campaign for independence but the governments of both Theresa May and Boris Johnson have refused requests for a second poll, citing the fact that the referendum of 2014 was supposed to be a once in a generation event. That position might be tenable so long as opinion polls do not show a clear majority in favour of change but it could not be maintained indefinitely if opinion polls were to show continued pressure in Scotland for independence.[1] Resisting such pressure could eventually run the risk of attempts of a non-constitutional type to force the issue. That would be disastrous and an outcome that anyone familiar with similar consequences elsewhere – and particularly with the history of Ireland in mind – should want to avoid. All countries, unfortunately, have a wilder element in their populations that can use a political problem to create mayhem. This was evident in Northern Ireland during the 'troubles'. Scotland is a peaceful country with a government that prioritises law and order. Hopefully that would not happen here but it would be unwise, by continually denying pressure for a referendum, to provide any excuse for it. One has to accept that one of the main causes of such pressure is that Scotland, for long periods in the recent past, has been governed by a party in Westminster it did not vote for.

The Scottish First Minister has made it plain that, although she wants a second referendum, she wants it in accordance with the constitution. The experience of Spain, where the government of Catalonia held a referendum in defiance of the Spanish constitution and the government in Madrid, with many unionists in Catalonia boycotting the poll, shows the mess that can result. In the meantime, the intervention of the coronavirus pandemic has monopolised attention and pushed the constitutional issue away from many people's minds.

The 2021 election to the Scottish Parliament, however, has resulted in increased votes for the SNP and the Green Party, both favouring independence, which only increases the pressure for a referendum. The SNP government does not have an overall majority on its own and, had it achieved this, that would have strengthened its position even more in pressing for a referendum. The UK government might, therefore, try to use this as some justification for continuing to refuse. But, with the support of the Greens, there can be little doubt that legislation for a referendum would be passed by the Scottish Parliament and, if the UK Parliament tried to block it, the matter could end up in the courts – a situation that should be avoided if at all possible.

Under the system of proportional representation that applies in Scotland, it is very difficult – indeed, it was thought to be virtually impossible – for any one party to gain an over-all majority in the Parliament, although the SNP managed to achieve this in the Parliament of 2011. When compared to elections to the UK Parliament, Scottish elections under the additional member system of proportional voting are, there-fore, a much better indication of the feelings of the electorate but they are by no means a completely accurate guide. Even with this PR system, therefore, a majority of seats does not necessarily reflect a majority of the popular vote. And there may be those who voted for the SNP or the Green Party who did so for other reasons and do not want independence. It cannot be assumed, therefore, that the election result would indicate a clear majority for independence in a referendum.

There can be no doubt, however, that the EU referendum of 2016 brought about a major change in circumstances for Scotland. Membership of the European Union was a major constitutional issue – the decision of the UK government was to leave, following a narrow majority of 51.9 per cent on a turnout of 72 per cent, but in contrast Scotland voted against leaving by 62 per cent on a turnout of 67 per cent. The Scottish vote to remain was, therefore, a more convincing result than the UK one for leave. Not a single Scottish local authority area showed a majority to leave. This clearly has major implications for politics in Scotland. Northern Ireland also voted to remain but not with quite such a convincing result as Scotland, while Wales, along with England voted to leave.

Effect on Trade

Among the implications for Scotland, the most obvious is the effect on trade. Just under half of Scotland's overseas exports go to the EU and they have grown by 4.1 per cent a year over the last five years. This compares with an average growth of 1.3 per cent to the rest of the world. Scotland's exports to the EU are worth more than those to North America, the Middle East, Asia, Africa and Australasia combined. Any barrier, even a modest one, to Scotland's EU trade is, therefore, likely to be damaging. Now that a last-minute agreement has been reached between the UK government and the EU Commission, the worst threat of a no-deal that would have been particularly damaging has been removed but it will only become clear with time what the consequences of the new agreement will be. There is to be free trade in goods although, so far, this is not straightforward, as the difficulties for companies trying to export and import in meeting regulatory requirements and dealing with increased bureaucracy have shown. The clearest example of this has been in the case of Scottish shellfish. Moreover, the agreement does not provide for free trade in services, where, outside the EU, trade with the single market will depend on agreed regulatory alignment. It is still not clear how far there will be agreement on this. Even with goods, apart from the greatly increased bureaucracy at customs posts, there are new customs posts for trade with Northern Ireland. The effect on the UK as a whole is not dissimilar from Scotland but, in England and Wales with a majority voting to leave the EU, it must be assumed that they accept the consequences.

However, Scotland's trade with the rest of the UK at £51.2 billion (in 2018) is much greater than the £33.8 billion with the EU and accounts for around 60 per cent of all Scottish exports. This has led those who oppose independence to say that it would be foolish for Scotland to put this at risk by leaving the UK and that this is more important than trying to safeguard European trade by applying to rejoin the EU as an independent country. This was an issue that did not arise at the time of the 2014 Scottish referendum. It was assumed then that the UK would remain a member of the EU – indeed, unionists argued that Scotland, as an independent state, might lose the advantage it had in trade with both the UK and the EU, since it could take years to rejoin the EU. But those who favoured independence argued that, if Scotland and the UK both remained in the EU, as was then expected, even if Scotland left the UK, since Scotland would still be in the EU's single market before becoming a full EU member state, trade with the rest of the UK and with the EU would continue much as before. Brexit has, therefore, resulted in a major and important change in Scotland's trade prospects and poses a dilemma that did not previously exist – how far the damage to the economy from leaving the EU through Brexit compares with damage from leaving the UK and rejoining the EU single market. This will depend not only on how the UK's post-Brexit trade arrangements work out, if Scotland remains part of the UK, but on what arrangements can be made for trade with the rest of the UK if Scotland becomes independent.

There is, however, an important difference in the type of trade Scotland does with the EU and with the rest of the UK. Scotland has become, like the rest of the UK, predominantly a service-based economy. Services now account for 75 per cent of activity in the Scottish economy compared with only 11 per cent for manufacturing. This contrasts with the 1960s when manufacturing accounted for a third or more of the economy's output. The move towards a service economy has resulted in greater dependence on the UK market. A lot of the services that are now so important to the economy by their nature cannot readily be exported across an international border. So, according to the University of Strathclyde's Fraser of Allander Institute, despite the reduced share of manufacturing in the economy, it still accounts for more international exports than services – £18 billion compared with £12.2 billion. Any policy to increase Scotland's overseas exports, therefore, must take account of the structure of the economy. It is not a matter of simply trying to exchange markets between the rest of the UK and those in the EU. If Scotland were to become independent, a change in the structure of the economy with an emphasis on growth of manufacturing products and on exportable services, such as international finance and tourism, would be necessary to increase exports to Europe and elsewhere.

As part of the EU, the UK also had the benefit of all the trade deals negotiated with third countries by the EU. Because the EU is the world's largest trading block with a population of some 440 million, it was in a very strong position in such negotiations. The UK will now lose the benefit of all these deals and will have to negotiate afresh. Brexiteers seem to think they can do better. That, of course, remains to be seen but it seems improbable, especially as the world – and especially the United States when it was led by President Trump – seemed to be moving more towards protection and away from globalisation. It is not yet clear how far this will remain policy during President Biden's presidency.

Investment

Trade prospects also have a major bearing on investment in the Scottish economy. Scotland has been one of the most successful parts of the UK in attracting investment from overseas, notably from the United States and the Far East. Those responsible in Scottish Enterprise and the Scottish government have put considerable energy into attracting such investment. Their success has often been dependent on unrestricted access to the EU single market, which was seen as a crucial advantage by many potential investors. This together with the long-recognised rule of law, absence of corruption and the English language are the clearest benefits cited by them. This latter applies particularly to companies from North America but English has become such an international language that many firms from other countries also find it easier to locate in an English-speaking country than elsewhere in Europe.

Scotland has had need of such investment because the amount that could be generated from domestic sources was insufficient to maintain full employment. The older industries – shipbuilding, heavy engineering, steel, textiles and coal mining – which once dominated the economy have been in precipitate decline over the last half century, so that a major effort was required to restructure the economy. Indeed, the very success of Scotland's early industrialisation created a greater need for restructuring than applied to most other economies. The attraction of overseas investment was, therefore, a crucial and indispensible part of the policy. Brexit, even a soft Brexit, will make this more difficult and even companies presently in the UK, whether British or foreign-owned, may, in time, see attractions in moving to the much larger European market. A lot will depend on how the Christmas 2020 agreement negotiated between the UK government and the EU works out. It remains to be seen whether this allows some of the benefits of membership of the single market to be retained.

It was in recognition of the potential damage to trade and investment from leaving the EU that the Scottish government submitted proposals to the government in Westminster in 2016 that would have enabled Scotland, while still part of the UK, to remain in the EU single market.[2] This was always a long shot and would almost certainly have necessitated some sort of checks at the Scottish–English border but, especially in view of the different referendum result in Scotland, the Westminster government should at least have given it the courtesy of a proper examination and discussion. It was, however, simply brushed aside. It is ironic, therefore, that, in the fraught discussions about Northern Ireland to avoid a hard border with the Irish Republic – something very similar to what the Scottish government had proposed – is to be accepted for Northern Ireland. In effect, the Northern Ireland protocol means that there will be a border in the Irish Sea so that Northern Ireland can remain free of impediments on trade with the Irish Republic. For a time, this seemed to have been put at risk by the admission from the Secretary of State for Northern Ireland that the UK's Internal Market Bill would result in some parts of this agreement being broken with assurances that trade between Northern Ireland and the UK will be free of any restriction. The future of this arrangement at the time of writing still seems rather uncertain, although it was apparently rectified in the latest agreement with the EU, which resulted in trade between Northern Ireland and the rest of the UK being subject to customs checks and, if necessary, duties.

Leaving the EU, especially against the wishes of Scottish people, as the result in the EU referendum made clear, is, therefore, a major change in circumstances and, in the view of many, that is sufficient to justify a second Scottish referendum, despite assurances given at the time of the last one that it would be a once in a generation event. It needs to be recognised that, in 2014, a decision to leave following the referendum of that year would not have resulted in any impediment to Scotland's trade with the rest of the UK. That is no longer so. If Scotland leaves the UK and seeks to have a renewed link with the EU, there would now have to be a trade border with the rest of the UK. This would have implications for Scottish businesses trading with the rest of the UK and, of course, for businesses in the rest of the UK trading with Scotland but it could result in preserving Scottish–EU trade links and might encourage EU-related international investment in Scotland.

What Kind of Referendum?

If a referendum does take place, its result, at the time of writing, looks far from clear. Until the middle of 2020, polls had shown a consistent majority of around 55 per cent for independence and one poll put the majority at 58 per cent. But, in the early part of 2021, there seemed to be a change, caused partly perhaps by problems within the SNP. If there is still a majority for leaving the UK, it is unlikely to be overwhelming and could easily change. There are many important issues to be considered and, as leaving the EU has increasingly shown, leaving the UK would be far from a simple matter. Indeed, after more than 300 years of union, it could be more difficult and disruptive than leaving the EU after only 47 years. It may be that, when some of the implications become clear – such as a hard border with the rest of the UK and a difficult budgetary situation that is likely to last for some years – support for independence will fall away. Campaigns for and against independence could change things considerably but, until 2021, a YES vote in a referendum looked quite likely and is still quite possible.

Scottish independence would be a major constitutional issue that would affect the whole of the UK. Inevitably, therefore, a Scottish referendum raises questions: whether it should require more than a wafer-thin majority for a change to take place; whether other parts of the UK that will be affected should have any say; whether Scots living outside Scotland should have a vote; whether the referendum should contain a question on federalism of the UK, as an alternative to independence. This latter could give Scotland more power over policy but preserve the union. It has also been suggested that there should be not one referendum but two – the first on the principle of independence and the second after negotiation to see whether, when the full implications are known, independence was still supported.[3] These are important matters and similar issues were discussed at some length in Canada at the time of the Quebec referendum. Eventually, however, a straight majority was applied there in its two referenda.

The Size of Majority

The importance of the issue to both Scotland and the UK means that it is greatly to be hoped that the result of the referendum should be really decisive – perhaps a 60 per cent majority or more for whatever the outcome, whether leaving or staying. Anything less could result in the referendum being extremely divisive, just as the UK's EU referendum proved to be, perhaps even more so. To decide to break up the UK on a 50+1 per cent majority would be likely to lead to a lot of ill feeling, demands for a repeat poll and countless difficulties. Moreover, a substantial majority voting to leave the UK would also make it less likely that public opinion would swing against the result if economic and political difficulties were encountered afterwards. This could lead to serious disappointment in Scotland.

In the 1979 referendum on Scottish devolution, the Cunningham amendment to the legislation required not only an outright majority to vote for change but for that majority also to be at least 40 per cent of the whole electorate. In the event, this latter condition was not satisfied and the Devolution Act was not implemented, although slightly more people voted for devolution than against it on a turnout of 64 per cent. A referendum on Scottish independence would involve a much greater constitutional change than one on devolution and a condition requiring something like 40 per cent of the whole electorate to vote for change could guard against having to implement a marginal result. But the Cunningham amendment was much resented in Scotland in 1979 and, in view of the rules applied to subsequent referenda in the UK, it seems pointless to think of it being repeated in any new referendum. The subsequent 1997 Scottish devolution referendum, the 2014 Scottish independence referendum (both of which were decided by the population actually living in Scotland) and the UK's 2016 EU referendum all required only a straight majority. Of these, the EU 2016 referendum had the closest result and, if something like the Cunningham amendment had applied, the UK might not have left the EU.

With these precedents it seems inevitable that a bare majority of those living in Scotland, whatever their place of birth and, therefore, most affected by the result, would be taken as decisive. But compared with 2014, one might expect the UK government to concern itself more closely with the ground rules than they did on that occasion. While there would be many in Westminster and in other parts of the UK who would regret a decision by Scotland to leave the UK, an attempt simply to continue to refuse consent for such a referendum could even result in greater support for it in Scotland, where people would feel that their democratic aspirations were being denied.

At the time of writing, it is very hard to predict what the result of such a referendum might be. A third of the Scottish population probably have a continuing strong loyalty to the UK and would not want to see Scotland leave under any circumstances; a further third are probably convinced nationalists, who would vote for independence even if it could be shown that it would be damaging economically; the remaining voters could swing either way and it is at them that any reasoning about Scotland's future should be mainly directed.

It is important that, whatever the decision, it should be based on a proper understanding of the issues involved, as the EU referendum was not. For the 2014 referendum, the Scottish government published a White Paper – *Scotland's Future* – and, although it was widely criticised, not least for the paucity of economic and financial analysis, it was at least a substantial document that attempted to deal with a large number of issues. Nothing similar was produced by the UK government for the EU referendum and there was much mendacity and even lies put forward in the claims of the Leave supporters.

Could Federalism be the Answer?

There are those who have suggested that an additional question should be in the referendum offering a proper federal constitution and that this could be the answer to the UK's constitutional problem, while avoiding many of the difficulties that would arise with independence. This has long been a policy supported by the Liberal Democrats and has attracted support in the Labour Party as well. It was suggested by Kezia Dugdale when she was leader of the Scottish Labour Party. It now has support also from Gordon Brown and, it would seem, from Keir Starmer.[4] City mayors in the north of England are also showing interest in such ideas and it is quite likely that, when the Labour Party next forms a government, major constitutional change could be part of its agenda. But the present UK government has never shown any interest in it and David Cameron, then UK Prime Minister, decided it should be a straight choice between independence and the status quo for the 2014 referendum. This was despite the SNP having suggested devo-max or federalism as options, along with independence and the status quo.

Several distinguished authors have written advocating a federal constitution, notably Jim Gallagher, a former director general for devolution in the UK Cabinet Office, and Andrew Blick.[5] Ben Thomson, in his 2020 book, *Scottish Home Rule*, has cogently argued the case for what he defines as Home Rule.[6] This latter has many of the characteristics of federalism but stops short of a federal constitution for the whole UK. It is possible that, if a UK government eventually accepts the need for a referendum, it may want a federal scheme as an alternative to independence, if it thinks that the political situation in Scotland would otherwise result in a vote leading to Scotland leaving the UK.

Federalism, however, would not be without serious problems. It could be either a federation of four countries, England, Scotland, Wales and Northern Ireland, in which case England, with 85 per cent of the population, would dominate to a degree that meant the smaller countries would tend to be outvoted on any issue of importance. Or it could be a federation of the three smaller countries and the English regions. This would achieve a better balance and, in Jim Gallagher's proposal, the English regions would have somewhat lesser powers than Scotland, Wales and Northern Ireland, probably without the power of legislate. But, although there is discontent in parts of England about their lack of power over decisions, when a devolution referendum was held during the last Labour government's time in the north-east of England, the region thought most likely to be in favour, it was overwhelmingly rejected by the electorate. This may now have changed and the resistance of the northern mayors, notably Andy Burnham in Manchester, at the time of the COVID restrictions, when they considered the financial arrangements unsatisfactory, may be a sign that opinion in the north of England is changing. But a major constitutional upheaval of the kind that would be involved still seems likely to be a long way off. Indeed, apart from the north-east, Yorkshire, the north-west and the south-west, many people in England might have difficulty in saying to which region they belonged.

There are also issues that would have to be decided over how such a federation would work. Presumably the intention would be, as Ben Thomson argues, to devolve most tax-raising powers, although it should be remembered that, in most federal countries, taxes are divided between the federal government and the states. In the US for example, the federal government is responsible for 64 per cent of all the taxes raised, with the remainder being the responsibility of the states and local authorities. Some key public expenditure is also the responsibility of the federal government. This provides some automatic support for the poorer members of the federation and helps to ensure cohesion. Similar arrangements apply in other federations. As will be shown in Chapter 10, the absence of such a mechanism is one of the reasons that there have been serious problems in the eurozone. Indeed, it can credibly be argued that such arrangements are necessary for a monetary union to work successfully.

Ben Thomson suggests a social cohesion fund, based on a needs assessment in each member state, to equalise standards in such major areas of public expenditure as healthcare, education and social security. This would certainly be necessary in the UK, given the very wide disparities in wealth and income levels, if the same standard of provision of public services was to be maintained throughout the country. If this approach is adopted, it should be done for the regions of England as well as the three smaller nations. A needs assessment, however, is not a straightforward matter – it is bound to involve a good deal of subjective judgement leaving scope for argument. It must be doubted if Ben Thomson's suggested arrangement would be enough to enable a UK federal system to work smoothly. Some have also suggested a reformed second chamber to replace the House of Lords, rather like the US Senate, in which the nations and regions of the UK would be represented. This would certainly be welcome – reform of the House of Lords is long overdue and has been an issue for the best part of 100 years – but this scale of change in the constitution would be unlikely to be agreed anytime soon. It may be that the opportunity for a major reform of this kind has been overtaken by the situation in Scotland, where the strength of feeling demands that a referendum should be held more urgently than the time it would take for any major constitutional reform of the UK to be enacted.

The Implications for the Rest of the UK

The effect of Scottish independence on the remainder of the UK has already been referred to. The Scottish population is only 5.5 million out of a UK total of 67 million but the remainder of the UK would nevertheless be diminished. This raises several really important questions. For example, how would it affect the UK's defence capability, especially as, assuming that the SNP policy does not change, it would be expected to lead to the closure of the UK's nuclear base on the Clyde? Indeed, this is one of the strong bargaining levers that Scotland could deploy in any negotiation. Could it even put the UK's permanent seat on the United Nations Security Council at risk? Decisions that affect the whole world now depend on relations between the United States and other major powers such as China, Russia, India, Brazil and Japan. There must be people in those other nations who do not see why Britain should still have a permanent place on the Security Council rather than, say, India or Japan. Despite these issues, any attempt to widen the referendum to include the electorate in other parts of the UK would certainly be resented in Scotland. It would have no precedent in previous referenda and UK citizens in the EU lost a court battle for the right to vote in 2016.

The world has become a more unsettled and worrying place with an increasingly aggressive Russia and a nationalistic China. Russian planes periodically probe UK airspace. There can be no doubt that President Putin welcomed a weakening of the EU as a result of the UK's decision to leave, even if he did not, as is now being suggested, attempt to influence the result. For similar reasons, he would probably also welcome Scottish independence, as he would see it as weakening the UK. Relations with China are also bad as a result of a more aggressive attitude there, following the British decision to reduce Huawei's role in the 5G network and the troubles in Hong Kong. These are matters that could affect not just the UK's influence in the world but also its security, including that of Scotland if it became independent. The world is now dominated by several very large states seeking a more important role in international affairs. This is another indication, if one were needed, of the importance of the EU, not just in trade negotiations but in international affairs generally and, if Scotland becomes independent, that points to allying itself to the EU. But these issues would also no doubt be used by unionists to emphasise the importance of maintaining the integrity of the UK.

Against these arguments, there is the fact that the EU referendum has resulted in Scotland leaving the EU against the wishes of its electorate. The consequences are likely to be damaging to Scotland's economy, especially in the longer term, as it would affect Scotland's ability to export to its main international market and reduce its attractiveness for investment to both domestic and international companies. At the present time, there is also a widespread feeling that Scotland's interests are not sufficiently understood or taken account of by the UK government. This is also a charge that the north of England could put to the government. It has after all suffered more than Scotland economically in recent years. But the existence of the SNP, together with the Scottish government and Parliament, give it a particular focus in Scotland.

A Confirmatory Referendum after the Implications of Independence are Clear

If a referendum is held, as may become inevitable, perhaps there is a case for Sir John Major's proposal of two referenda – one on the principle of independence and the second to ensure that the public still favour it when they see what would be involved. Of course Sir John was proposing it in the expectation that the second referendum might result in the proposals for independence being rejected but it would at least ensure that the public knew what to expect from independence and help to guard against a strong adverse reaction afterwards. If such a second vote had been a requirement after the EU referendum, when the full implications of leaving the EU had become clear, it might well have resulted in Brexit being rejected.

Scottish independence would undoubtedly be a major upheaval, with serious consequences for a lot of people. The trouble with Sir John Major's suggestion, however, is that it could encourage those in the UK most opposed to Scottish independence to make the difficulties before the second referendum was held seem even greater to increase the chances of a NO vote.

Options for an independent Scotland

If the Scottish people decide in favour of independence in a referendum, a choice would then be required over what kind of independence that should be. The following paragraphs set out a number of options.

There are some in the SNP who appear to want Scotland not to be part of the UK and not to have anything to do with the EU either. A second possibility would be to combine independence with being as close as possible to the UK, perhaps remaining in the UK single market and customs union and continuing to use sterling. A third possibility – and the one most frequently quoted by SNP spokespeople – would be to leave the UK and apply for renewed membership of the EU as an independent country. Finally there is the option of membership of the European Economic Area (EEA) – like Norway, Iceland and Liechtenstein – which would give Scotland membership of the EU single market but not require it to be in the EU Customs Union. These will be examined in turn.

Scotland as Independent of the UK and with No Links to the EU

If Scotland became independent of the UK, ceased to be a member of the UK single market and did not have any trading arrangements with the EU, it would experience major trading difficulties. Maybe there are those who thought that a trading deal could be done with the United States. But that seemed fanciful, especially after the US under Donald Trump imposed increased duties on Scotch whisky. And, even if it were possible, it could only lead to Scotland accepting any conditions that the US decided on. Now that President Biden has been elected, he is expected to want to mend his links with both the EU and the UK. But it remains to be seen what agreement might be negotiated. Links with other countries, including those of the Commonwealth, would be on a basis that would require Scotland to accept whatever terms were offered. Investment on any scale would be most unlikely, as there would be barriers to trade both with the UK and the EU. It would surely be the worst outcome and a quick route to the country's impoverishment.

Retaining the UK Single Market

The second possible policy could enable economic links with the UK to be retained but without any influence on UK policies and, if sterling was retained as the currency, Scotland would be without any influence in its management. There are several countries that use the dollar on this basis but it means they have no national control over one of the main levers of economic policy. As regards its fiscal position, Scotland at present raises less from taxation than is spent on public expenditure in Scotland. This will be dealt with at greater length in the next chapter but it means that either taxes would have to rise or public expenditure be cut, leading to painful and unpopular decisions.

There are those who argue that, although Scotland has a weaker budgetary position than the UK as a whole at present, independence could change that. But they do not explain how this is to be done. It is doubtful if a reduction in Scotland's defence expenditure from the population share presently indicated as a part of the UK in 'Government Expenditure and Revenue Scotland' or reneging on the population's share of the national debt, which some people have proposed, would be sufficient, even if they were acceptable. It would be essential somehow to get the economy to grow faster, if the gap between expenditure and revenue was to be closed without either serious cuts or increased taxation. Scotland would have greater freedom to diverge from UK policies but it has more freedom now than the Scottish government has decided to use, probably because, as soon as there are differences from what is done by the UK, it attracts a lot of controversy and newspaper headlines of the kind 'Scotland More Heavily Taxed than the UK'. This could discourage investment and result in some wealthy individuals deciding to move elsewhere in the rest of the UK. There would be no supporting funds from the rest of the UK, as happens now with the Barnett formula, and, if monetary union with the rest of the UK was to be retained, there would be no ability to use the exchange rate to bring the economy into better balance. It is not easy to see how this situation would have advantages over remaining within the UK. It is possible, however, that, despite intentions to the contrary, the monetary union with the rest of the UK could not be maintained – just as was proved to be case when the Czech Republic and Slovakia separated. This could be painful but, as explained later, it could have some advantages.

Joining the EU as a Full Member

The third option of applying to join the EU as a member state after independence is the one favoured by most of those who argue for independence and is probably the one most likely to be followed, if Scotland becomes independent after a referendum. It would take some time, possibly years, but there should be no difficulty in meeting the economic requirements of the single market and customs union, as

Scotland has so recently been part of a member state that complied with EU treaties and conditions. It would require all existing member states to agree and there might be some political difficulties from any countries in the EU that were resisting secessionist movements in their own territory. They might use the size of the budget deficit, if it still existed at the time of application and was higher than permitted for eurozone members, as an argument for refusing membership or the fact that Scotland did not have its own currency, if it continued to use sterling. The most likely problem could arise with Spain and, in the worst case, Spain or any other state could exercise a veto. Even if some other members were quite enthusiastic to have Scotland as a member after the UK has left, it would require only the veto of one member state to block entry.

Member states of the EU are required to subscribe to the *acquis communautaire*, the accumulated legislation that governs the EU. Membership of the euro is a part of this and states joining would be expected in due course to adopt it as their currency. Only the UK, while it was a member, and Denmark had opt-outs but many states have still not joined the eurozone, even without formal opt-outs. Sweden, for example, joined the EU without an opt-out from the euro but put the issue to a referendum which rejected it. No one now expects any action to be taken to try to force Sweden to join. Six other countries – Poland, the Czech Republic, Hungary, Romania, Bulgaria and Croatia – continue to use their own currencies. There is a fairly widespread view that it was a mistake for Greece to join the euro and possibly it should have left when it was hit by the financial crisis. Indeed, the damage to Greece has been enormous and, in my view, it would have been better for the other countries to help Greece to leave the eurozone, with financial aid to restructure its debts, than to pay money to allow it to stay in. This would have enabled it to re-establish its own currency with the freedom to adjust its exchange rate to a level that helped the Greek economy to recover. Scotland, at present, would not meet the budgetary requirements for being a eurozone member, as its deficit would be above the maximum of 3 per cent of GDP, which is one of the conditions to be satisfied by members joining. And, if Scotland did become an EU member, although it might be expected to make membership of the eurozone a long-term aim, it could not be compelled to join.

Assuming Scotland was accepted for EU membership, it would retain the advantages it had until recently in trade with Europe and there is a good chance that it would be able to attract more investment, both international and domestic, than it will be able to do if it stays outside the EU as part of the UK. As pointed out in the last chapter, many of the companies that have invested in Scotland, since the UK joined what is now the EU in 1973, have made it clear that access to the EU market was a principal reason for doing so and, now that the UK has left, they may reduce their role in Scotland, if Scotland remains part of the UK. So inward investment might well increase compared with the status quo and there might even be companies that would consider moving to Scotland from the rest of the UK to get unrestricted access to the EU. But, on the other hand, there could also be some businesses presently in Scotland or thinking of coming for whom a hard border with the rest of the UK would be a deterrent. This is true in the financial sector, for which renewed membership of the EU single market could be seen as an advantage, but where some firms might move to the rest of the UK, if that was where their main market was (see Chapter 8). How large these effects might be and whether the advantages of being in the EU single market would outweigh the disadvantages of a hard border with the rest of the UK for firms seeking to invest is impossible to judge. They would only become clear after a number of years.

Clearly the disadvantage – and it is a major one – would be the effect on Scottish trade with the rest of the UK which, as explained in the first part of this book, is greater than the trade it does with the EU. Membership of the EU would, of course, require a hard border between Scotland and the rest of the UK, since the UK is outside the EU. The damage to Scottish–UK trade would be less than it would have been if the UK had not reached a free trade agreement for goods with the EU in the Christmas 2020 negotiations but the agreement does not apply to services. For Scotland, as an EU member state, it would still involve delays, checks and bureaucracy, which would be increasingly evident as the UK diverged from the EU on regulations. All this would add to the costs of trade with the rest of the UK. It would, therefore, be a major issue that supporters of the union would raise in any debate on Scotland's future.

There would have to be customs posts at all border crossing points with England, affecting trade in a way that has not happened since the Act of Union in 1707. This is what is happening now with Northern Ireland in line with the protocol negotiated as part of the UK–EU agreement. It would also mean that Scotland would have to adhere to the EU's regulatory arrangements on all goods and these might differ increasingly from those applied in the rest of the former UK, as the UK government develops its policies. The Brexiteers have made much of the freedom leaving the EU would give them to escape EU regulations, giving rise to the suggestion that it could become some kind of Singapore on Thames. This they claim as a major benefit but it remains to be seen what may actually happen and, therefore, how important it would be. Even if UK regulations remained very close to those of the EU, thereby facilitating trade between an independent Scotland as an EU member and the rest of the UK, they could change at any time in the future and Scotland would have no influence or control over that.

The Northern Ireland protocol is an attempt to mitigate these problems in the case of Northern Ireland and how it evolves may give some guidance to what might happen if Scotland becomes independent and an EU member. It is an attempt to solve the insoluble by avoiding a hard border between Northern Ireland and the Irish Republic, which would be an inevitable consequence if Northern Ireland simply left the EU single market along with the rest of the UK. Such a border, involving customs controls and checks, would be disruptive to trade within Ireland and damage the fragile peace that was brokered in the Good Friday agreement. If there is to be no border within the island of Ireland, in effect keeping Northern Ireland in the EU single market, there has, despite assurances to the contrary from the Prime Minister, to be a border between Northern Ireland and the rest of the UK. This has aroused much hostility, and some resort to violence, on the part of elements in the loyalist community. It remains to be seen how this will work in practice. The extent of the problem will of course depend on how far the UK departs from the rules of the EU single market both on tariffs and regulations. How the problem is mitigated, however, could set a precedent for negotiations between an independent Scotland in the EU and the rest of the UK. It could also be an indication of the likely hostility from those in Scotland who would want to avoid such a border with the rest of the UK.

Migration

There would also be difficulties over migration. It should be remembered that significant numbers of Italians came to Scotland between the wars and many Poles came during the Second World War. Both have made their homes here and are valuable members of the community. Arguably, because they shared the European culture and religion, this has made their assimilation easy. Since the 1960s there have been Indians and Pakistanis who have also settled and made their homes here. More recently still, substantial numbers again have come from Poland and from other eastern EU countries. The flow from the latter was especially large in the 1990s and early 2000s after their countries joined the EU. The UK government at that time could have temporarily restricted the numbers, as there was provision to do that under EU rules, but they did not do so. Now as Poland and the other countries have achieved improved economic growth, this flow has greatly diminished and many have returned to their own countries.

The Scottish government has made it clear that it would like to see more immigration because the present low birth rate combined with increased life expectancy is creating a serious demographic problem. They rightly see this as a major advantage of being a member state of the EU. The number of people of working age is a decreasing proportion of the population and they will have to bear the cost of supporting those in retirement who, as a result of advances in medical science, are living ever longer and increasing in number. Whether the elderly population have pensions from the state financed by taxation or private pensions does not affect this. The latter should give the elderly more income than if they rely on the state alone, but those in work and producing will always bear the cost of those who are not, whatever the funding mechanism may be.

Old people are heavily dependent on healthcare so that the demands on the health service will continue to rise faster than the country's GDP. This will be a major problem as the proportion of dependents in the economy increases and has, up to now, been eased by the number of staff that came from EU countries in Scotland's health service.

The UK never signed the Schengen Agreement, which provided for completely unrestricted movement of people between member states, but it was nevertheless required to allow migration from other EU member states. Scotland, like other member states, would have to subscribe to the four freedoms of the EU – movement of goods, services, people and capital. If it became independent, Scotland might, like Ireland, be able to remain in the common travel area of the UK and avoid having to accept the full implications of the Schengen Agreement. That, however, would require negotiation. These four freedoms were enshrined in the EU Single Act of 1986–87, the text of which said 'the internal market shall comprise an area without internal frontiers' and were given new impetus by the 1992 Programme and the Maastricht Treaty that established the European single market. UK Ministers have made it quite clear, however, that controlling the flow of migration from the EU was one of the main factors driving Brexit. The consequence of the UK policy is, therefore, likely to be fewer people coming from the EU, but the numbers coming from the Commonwealth and elsewhere will be unaffected and may actually increase.

If an independent Scotland joins the EU, some control over population movement from Scotland to England would therefore seem inevitable. Even if there was agreement to maintain the common travel area, UK Ministers would want to ensure that EU migrants could not simply use Scotland as some sort of back-door entry to the other countries of the UK. Again, that would require some control at the Scotland–England border either with passports or some other means of identification.

Agriculture and Fisheries

Another major advantage of leaving the EU claimed by the Brexiteers is that the UK would no longer have to accept the EU's common agricultural and fisheries policies. But, as these industries are discovering, it also ends their easy access to EU markets, something that is very important both for livestock and fish. The shellfish industry in particular is suffering from serious delays, which affect the freshness and, therefore, the value of the product, even if it gets market access.

If Scotland rejoined the EU, it would have to accept both of these policies but it would also regain the easy access to the EU market. If, however, it tried to negotiate special conditions to retain a larger share of the fish catch than would be available under the EU quota system by excluding other EU nations from Scottish waters in the North Sea, it is unlikely that it would be accepted as a member.

It has yet to be seen what the UK will do to replace the EU agricultural and fisheries policies. For agricultural policy, Conservative Ministers have given assurances that agriculture would continue to be supported but mainly by measures directed at environmental protection rather than by price or income support. There must be a serious danger, however, that the UK may gradually revert to the type of unprotected policy for agriculture that applied before World War II, when the UK depended on domestic agriculture for only about 30 per cent of food production, compared with around 60 per cent now. UK Ministers in both of the UK's major political parties have argued that policies – such as the EU single farm payment that has supported farmers' incomes – should be replaced. This is especially likely if the UK does a trade deal with the United States, which is keen to supply the UK market from its own huge farming businesses. This could seriously affect the rules ensuring the welfare of livestock and the quality of the ultimate product, both of which are governed by EU regulations to ensure high standards.

The EU's Common Agricultural Policy (CAP) undoubtedly has its flaws and involves rules and bureaucracy that farmers dislike but Scottish agriculture relies to a large extent on livestock production, for which access to the EU market is important. More than half the territory is primarily grazing land that is categorised by the EU as 'less favoured'. It can, therefore, like other such areas throughout Europe, take advantage of the EU Less Favoured Area Support Scheme (LFASS). This is very different from the leafy meadows in Oxfordshire or, indeed, much of southern England. It seems a reasonable conclusion that Scottish agriculture would do better and its less favoured areas would be more protected under the EU's Common Agricultural Policy than by any regime that the UK might introduce with a bias to the needs of England.

Fisheries are another matter. The Common Fisheries Policy (CFP) would have to be accepted. It is, however, greatly disliked by Scottish fishermen and resulted in many of them voting against membership of the EU. It probably caused many of them to be in favour of Brexit. The Scottish fishing industry is only a small part of the Scottish economy but it is of major importance to the north-east of Scotland and Shetland and, in the case of shellfish, to the west coast and the Hebrides. Leaving the CFP was seen by many fishermen, and therefore some politicians with constituencies in the north-east of Scotland, as one of the main advantages of Brexit. Fishermen were nervous that their interest would be brushed aside in any negotiation. And although, as a result of the Christmas agreement between the UK and the EU, they will have an improved share of the catch, many of them still regard the agreement as some kind of betrayal. The Scottish fishing industry, after all, sells much of its product in EU markets to which it still wants access and, as events have shown, that has now become not only more difficult but involves delays at the border that can affect the value and freshness of the product. To avoid this, it has been reported that some Scottish fishermen are now landing their catch in Denmark. Access to EU markets for Scottish fish would, of course, be safeguarded in any agreement on Scottish membership of the EU just as it was before the UK left.

The real problem with fishing is that modern vessels with their sophisticated techniques and equipment for tracking the fish are so efficient that the catch has reached the point where fish stocks could very easily be fished out and it could take very many years, if ever, for them to recover. Some years ago, there was already much concern that cod stocks were dangerously low. The main principle of EU fishing policy is that national boundaries are not recognised in the sea between member states and fishing is regulated by quotas for each country. Scottish fishermen argued that they could get a larger share of the catch if the UK, after leaving the EU, claimed its full territorial limits. Clearly this would not arise if Scotland rejoined the EU but there could then be implications for Scottish fishermen if they wanted to fish in English or Northern Irish waters.

The EU policy based on quotas allocated to each country has been difficult to operate, especially in a mixed fishery, such as for white fish, where inevitably a variety of species are caught at the same time. Even where the aim is to catch cod or haddock, for example, there may be a substantial bycatch of other fish. Fishing up to the quota for one species could mean exceeding it for others, with the result that there could be either massive discards or illegal landings. Both of these have been a feature of the industry in the past. Great efforts to stop this have been made by clamping down on illegal landings and by stopping discards. This has had some effect but, every year, the fishing organisations in each country have pressed their Ministers to try to get a larger quota in the annual CFP negotiations. The result has been that quotas frequently exceeded the recommendations of the scientists advising on what was necessary to preserve stocks. The EU's Common Fisheries Policy has been bureaucratic and certainly too centralised but, despite all its faults, it has been able to prevent a collapse in stocks.

Contribution to the EU Budget

Rejoining the EU would mean Scotland having to contribute to the EU budget. Leaving has meant that the UK no longer makes a contribution. This is an issue that the Brexiteers have made much of and the infamous bus slogan that claimed a saving of £350 million a week, though derided by many, drew attention to the issue. This was blatantly misleading because it did not take account of the UK's discount or the money that the UK got back from the EU budget for agriculture and for regional development. The net cost to the UK was £8.7 billion in 2018 or around 1 per cent of GDP, which compares with about 37 per cent of GDP paid in taxes to the UK exchequer. This amounts to a net cost per annum over the period 2014–20 of £117 per head for the whole UK, a figure most analysts consider to be dwarfed by the benefits in trade.

But the net cost varied considerably between the different countries of the UK. For England, it was £140 per head and, for Scotland, it was much less at £64. For Northern Ireland, it was £31 and Wales actually received more in payments from the EU than it paid, giving a net receipt of £164 per head.[1] One wonders if the people of Wales understood this when a majority there voted to leave the EU!

If Scotland was applying to become a member of the EU after independence, it could not expect to retain a part of the UK's discount, which amounted to £4.2 billion in 2018. The Scottish share of this has not been calculated and, in any case, circumstances have changed considerably since the discount was negotiated. A part of the reason for the discount was that the method then applied for contributions to the EU budget was thought to be unfair to the UK because they depended on import levies and tariffs that disadvantaged the UK and on a share of VAT. With a relatively small but efficient agriculture, the amount received through the Common Agricultural Policy would be much less than other large countries get. Now, however, contributions are predominantly based on each country's GDP and agricultural support, though still large, is no longer so dominant a part of the EU's expenditure.

The result, not unreasonably, is that the richer countries pay more than those that are poorer. Scotland's GDP per head would be well above the EU average so it could expect to be a net contributor, though it could receive substantial sums both for agriculture and for regional development. That the richer countries help the poorer not only helps the cohesion of the EU but also, in my view, makes economic sense. Just as it was right for the US to help Europe with Marshall Aid after the war because it could not expect countries impoverished by war to buy its exports, so helping the poorer member states of the EU, especially those in the east, will enable them, as they develop, to increase trade and buy more from the richer countries. Scotland could not, therefore, expect to benefit from the discount on the budgetary contribution, which Mrs Thatcher obtained for the UK, and would be a net contributor to the EU budget. If the contributions of other countries of similar size can be taken as a rough guide and, if it amounted to about 1 per cent of GDP or £1.8 billion, this could be offset by receipts of perhaps three quarters of a billion.

In summary therefore, if an independent Scotland chose to apply for renewed membership of the EU, it might take a considerable time for it to be accepted, probably some years. Once accepted, there would be a hard border with England. This would be inevitable, even with the free trade in goods negotiated in the Christmas 2020 agreement, and would involve hassle and customs checks that would affect both imports and exports with the remainder of the UK. It could also involve a restraint on free movement between Scotland and the rest of the UK – if only to prevent migrants using entry to Scotland as a backdoor to other UK countries. It would automatically have to accept the Common Agricultural Policy, from which it could benefit, but also the Common Fisheries Policy, which would be politically difficult for the fishing communities. Scotland could not expect to retain a share of the UK's discount on its contribution to the EU's budget. There would, however, be benefits to Scottish trade with the EU and Scotland would be better placed to encourage international investment.

Membership of the European Economic Area

If Scotland votes to become independent, the fourth option would be to apply to rejoin the European Free Trade Association (EFTA), which includes Norway, Iceland, Liechtenstein and Switzerland, and then seek to become a member of the European Economic Area (EEA), which also includes the EU. Membership, which dates from the EEA Agreement of 1994, would be a two-stage process. It is only open to member states of the EU and EFTA but Switzerland, although a member of EFTA, has never joined the EEA and has its own bilateral agreements with the EU. Scotland would, therefore, need to join EFTA first and then apply to join the EEA. This requires the agreement of all the other EEA members, including the three EFTA states that are members, and all 27 members of the EU. If there were to be any difficulties for Scotland, it is at this stage that they might arise. Such difficulties cannot be excluded but EEA membership would probably be less likely to incur the hostility of any member state concerned about secessionist movements in their own countries than if Scotland was seeking to join the EU itself. As an EEA member Scotland would be subject to the EFTA court on disputed matters and would have to contribute to the EU budget mainly to promote cohesion among the members, as Norway does, but not quite as much as it would as a full member state of the EU.

The EEA is a free trade area and importantly also provides membership of the EU single market. However, apart from the members of the EU itself, EEA countries are not within the Customs Union. This means that goods exported between members of the EEA, including those in the EU, are free of tariffs and they must comply with EU regulatory standards. The only goods that could be subject to tariffs are agricultural and fisheries exports since EFTA/EEA members are not included in the common policies for agriculture and fisheries and are, therefore, not in the single market for these products. But there is an obligation that 'contracting parties undertake to continue their efforts with a view to achieving progressive liberalisation of agricultural trade'.[2] Although tariffs or import levies are, therefore, payable, this could presumably be subject to some negotiation and would apply not only to exports from an EEA country to the EU or to other EEA members but also to imports from them. Indeed, agricultural protection in Norway is generally higher than in the EU and there have been complaints about tariffs being too high for cheese. Furthermore, because the three EEA countries are not in the EU Customs Union, they are not required to impose the EU external tariffs on goods imported from third countries, on which they are responsible for making their own arrangements.

This would give Scotland the advantages its government sought in its 2016 paper 'Scotland's Place in Europe'.[3] As an EEA member, Scottish trade to the EU would have to conform to the EU regulations and standards that apply to all members of the single market but would have duty-free access to the EU market for goods and services exported from Scotland. Export trade would be subject, however, to the certificate of origin rules so that goods would not escape import duties if they, or a major part of them, came from countries outside the single market. Normally, if a product is at least 60 per cent manufactured in the EEA member state, it would be free of any duty. This would be complicated and involve much bureaucracy. It could restrict trade in Scottish products that contained significant parts manufactured outside the EEA – for example, in other parts of the UK – but it would be workable as the example of Norway shows. Even with this restriction, exporting Scottish goods to the EU would be much easier than if it was either on its own or as part of the UK outside the EU.

How the UK's free trade agreement in goods of Christmas 2020 would affect this is, at present, not clear. Presumably, certificate of origin rules would still apply but goods that were shown to be from or partly from the rest of the UK would be exempt from duties and quotas, so long as they conformed to EU standards. This would certainly make it much easier for Scotland, as an EEA member, since such a large part of its trade is with the rest of the UK.

A major benefit, which would not apply to the rest of the

UK, is that the EEA also provides for membership of the EU internal market for services, which has involved the removal of non-tariff barriers to trade in services. In consequence, because the EEA is part of the EU regulatory union, service providers have to comply with EU law, even if they do not trade with the EU. Free trade in services could be especially important for Scotland's financial sector and it could prove a major benefit if it resulted in the relocation of some financial businesses from the rest of the UK, just as has happened in Ireland (see Chapter 8).

For Scotland, EEA membership would have the advantage of combining full membership of the EU single market with the ability to negotiate its own bilateral trading arrangements with other countries. There would still have to be a border with the rest of the UK, with checks and customs posts, but Scotland might be able to retain many of the advantages it presently has from being in the UK single market. It could also mean that, if the rest of the UK had special deals with the US or with Commonwealth countries, Scotland could negotiate such deals as well although, if such goods were re-exported to Europe, they would be subject to the certificate of origin rules. In this respect, it would be less disruptive than if Scotland joined the EU as a full member.

Members of the EEA are not expected to adopt the euro and are, therefore, not in the eurozone. Nor would Scotland be governed by the EU's common agricultural and fishing policies. For both, Scotland would have to have its own policies. For its agricultural products and for fish, however, access to European markets would be important and negotiation would be needed. This might well require agreement to allow some access for fishermen of EU countries to Scottish waters, as applies now for Norway.

Scotland's chances of securing international investment and its prospects for domestic investment would be good, possibly better than as a full member of the EU, as it would not only have single market access to the EU but also, as a result of the Christmas 2020 agreement, free trade for goods with the rest of the UK. Furthermore, trade in services that was only between Scotland and the rest of the UK would be governed by whatever arrangements were agreed bilaterally. This could go some considerable way to safeguarding the large amount of trade Scotland does with the rest of the UK.

A disadvantage, as compared with full EU membership, would be that Scotland would be strictly a rule taker but EFTA states are involved in the negotiations that lead to most single market legislation. Single market legislation does not have a direct effect in EFTA states, which have to introduce EU law into their domestic legal order. This is then subject to the jurisdiction of the EFTA court and not the European Court of Justice. As it would not be a full member of the EU, Scotland would have no EU commissioner and not be present at discussions determining EU policies. This has been regarded by Brexiteers as ruling out UK membership of the EEA. But, even if Scotland was a full EU member, as a small state among 27 other members, one has to be realistic about the amount of influence it would have in such matters. Furthermore, there would be no requirement to be part of moves towards closer political integration.

There seem to be clear advantages in Scotland joining the EEA rather than seeking full membership of the EU, if it decides to become independent. It could probably be achieved much more quickly than EU membership and it would give the possibility of maintaining more flexible trade with the rest of the UK. It would give Scotland membership of the EU single market, which Brexit is causing it to lose. If Scotland decided that, in the end, however, it wanted to be a full EU member state, it would take time, probably some years, for Scotland to be accepted and EEA membership in the meantime could be seen both by the Scottish government and the EU Commission as a staging post on the way to that goal. It would also give time for Scottish trade to adjust to greater participation with the EU while reducing its dependence on the rest of the UK. Once a member of the EEA, Scotland might decide that it had gained the advantages from the single market that it wanted and that full membership of the EU was unnecessary at least for several years.

Deficit, debt, the sharing of assets and options for the currency

If Scotland does become an independent state following a referendum, would it be prosperous or ensnared in economic difficulties? Many who support independence argue that small states are more economically successful than large ones. This view was endorsed in the report of the Sustainable Growth Commission – a body with a distinguished membership drawn from business and the universities as well as from politics, which was set up by the Scottish National Party.[1]

There is some truth in this. With high rates of emigration and an income per head only about half the average for the UK, Ireland was very poor at the time it became independent. But it now has an income per head as measured by GNP at least comparable to the UK.[2] Would it have done anything like as well if it had remained part of the UK? That seems extremely unlikely. Would Denmark be as prosperous if it was part of Germany? In general, the Scandinavian countries, though small in population, have done extremely well economically. It may be that the government of a small state is better placed to be nimble in the policies it applies and small states often do not carry the same burdens as large ones – for example, in defence expenditure.

But it does not follow that all small countries do well and small size is certainly not by itself enough to ensure prosperity.

Much will depend on the wisdom or otherwise of government policies, particularly in trade and encouragement of investment. Ireland had a very poor economic performance for the first 30 or so years of its independence. It was not until the end of the 1950s, under the leadership of its then Taoiseach, Sean Lemass, that the government started to put the right measures in place to promote economic growth.

In Scotland's case, prospects would be heavily dependent on how it handled its decisions on trade with the UK on the one hand and trade with the EU on the other. Brexit has affected this in ways that could not be foreseen at the time of the 2014 referendum. The choices open to Scotland for trading relationships were discussed in the last chapter but an independent Scotland would face other formidable issues. Some of these were addressed in the report of the Sustainable Growth Commission. If independence is to happen, the Scottish government needs to have a properly worked-out plan setting out the issues so that the electorate can take a decision based on some knowledge of what would be in store, rather than one based largely on assertions and emotion. Without this, there is a serious risk of disillusionment afterwards and a strong political reaction. But once a decision in favour of independence is taken, there would be no going back. The work of the Sustainable Growth Commission, therefore, needs to be updated and then published. It was absurd that this important document was only published electronically. It should have been published properly to enable wider discussion and debate. Brexit continues to raise many issues that could not be examined when the report was written. Further work is therefore necessary. So far, there has been insufficient attention paid to the Commission's recommendations and it would appear that they have been neither accepted nor properly planned for.

Some of the most important issues are: the existing budgetary deficit, which was over 8 per cent of GDP in 2019–20 before the COVID pandemic's full effect was felt and is now much higher because of it, as shown in the Scottish government's own publication 'Government Expenditure and Revenue Scotland 2020–21'; the division of liabilities such as the national debt held by the UK of which Scotland should have a share; and the likelihood also of a deficit on the current account of the balance of payments. A decision would be needed on the currency to be used – whether Scotland would continue to use the pound sterling, start to use the euro or introduce a new currency of its own. There would also need to be a decision on the division of assets such as the UK's foreign exchange reserves, defence forces and the arrangements for defence.

This is a daunting list. Something at least of the thinking behind the plans to tackle these issues should be set out before any referendum, if the electorate is to take a decision with proper understanding and knowledge of the implications. The white paper that preceded the 2014 referendum had its share of weaknesses. On the currency, in particular, there was a lack of clarity, which may have affected the final result. But, unlike the UK's EU referendum, where there was no such document, it was at least published. The rest of this chapter attempts to deal with these issues.

Balancing the Budget

'Government Expenditure and Revenue Scotland 2020–21' shows a gap with expenditure exceeding revenue in 2019–20 by some 8.8 per cent of GDP, including a geographical share of North Sea revenues, while, for the UK as a whole, the gap, which had been large following the financial crisis, was 2.5 per cent. This has now increased in 2020–21 to a deficit for Scotland of 22.4 per cent and for the UK to 14.2 per cent (see Table 1).[3] For both Scotland and the UK, the deficit had risen slightly even in 2019–20 compared with the previous year, possibly as a consequence of COVID, but the full effect of that did not come through until 2020–21. The result is that the deficit is now very high and, although it can be expected to fall again after the pandemic has passed, the increase for Scotland was larger than for the UK as a whole and it remains to be seen whether it will fall again to the levels normally seen before the crisis.

Table 1: Net Fiscal Balance: Scotland
As a percentage of GDP

	2018–19	2019–20	2020–21
Excluding North Sea revenue	-9.2	-10.0	-23.8
Including North Sea revenue (geographical share)	-7.7	-8.8	-22.4
UK	-1.8	-2.6	-14.2

This issue has attracted a lot of attention and is clearly important.[4] What COVID has done is simply to make what was previously a serious issue very much worse. Supporters of the union say it shows Scotland would be much worse off if it was independent since, even if the budget deficit returned to the levels common before the pandemic, it would have to be eliminated, by either raising taxes or cutting public expenditure – and the latter would require a long period of renewed austerity. Some have asserted that it shows Scotland being supported by England. On the nationalist side, there have been those that have said this only shows that Scotland has a deficit as part of the union of the UK and that, with independence, the position would be quite different. That is no doubt true but the respects in which it would be different have not been adequately analysed.

Added to all this will be the massive amount the UK has had to borrow in 2020 because of the coronavirus pandemic. This was forecast by the Office for Budget Responsibility to be £394 billion or 19 per cent of GDP for the fiscal year 2020–21, the highest figure since the Second World War and may well be higher when the full consequences of COVID become clear. While interest rates remain exceptionally low, this is not a major issue but, if they were to rise, as is to be expected eventually, and if the debt had to be refinanced, the interest payments would amount to a major additional cost to the Scottish budget.

The fact is, however, that, within a nation state, particularly within a monetary union, some parts of the union will usually be in surplus and others in deficit, as it is only the position of the state as a whole that matters. At the time of writing, the latest published figures for the countries and regions of the UK are for 2018–19 (see Table 2). These show that almost all the regions of England, plus Wales and Northern Ireland, as well as Scotland, were in budget deficit – the only English regions in surplus were London, the South-East and the Eastern Region.

Scotland's deficit in 2019–20 was £15.8 billion, even including a geographic share of North Sea oil revenues and this rose to £36.3 billion in 2020–21. But, on a per head of population basis, Scotland's deficit in the earlier year of 2018–19 of £2,800 per head was exceeded by Northern Ireland (nearly twice as much), Wales, the North-east, North-west and West Midlands and, although the figures will now be larger for all regions, the pattern is likely to have remained the same. So it is not simply a question of Scotland being supported by the UK but all the regions of the UK being supported by the three in surplus. This simply points to the very serious regional imbalance within the UK and the exceptional dominance of London and the South-East. This is greater than the imbalance in most other European countries and it is something that the UK government needs to address if, in the long run, there is not to be serious discontent in disadvantaged parts of the UK. It suggests that, if the three surplus regions were excluded, the rest of the country would probably have to endure some kind of tight fiscal policy to restore balance or reduce their deficits by devaluing their currency to stimulate growth.

Table 2: Net Fiscal Balance per head 2018–19
by countries and regions of the UK
£ per head including North Sea Revenues (geographic share)

Country /Region	2018–19	2019–20
North East	-4,064	-4,164
North West	-2,780	-3,098
Yorkshire & Humber	-2,090	-1,241
East Midlands	-1,323	-1,497
West Midlands	-2,545	-2,928
East of England	+661	+568
London	+4,350	+4,025
South East	+2,375	+2,136
South West	-999	-1,100
Wales	-4,307	-4,566
Scotland	-2,482	-2,800
Northern Ireland	-4,996	-5,440
United Kingdom	-623	-863

Source: Office of National Statistics

There is, however, an important difference between the position of Scotland, on the one hand, and Northern Ireland, Wales and most of the English regions, on the other. Scotland's contribution to revenue in 2020–21 on a per-head basis at £11,496 is only £382 below the UK average of £11,878; indeed it was the highest in the UK after London, the South-East and Eastern England, whereas public expenditure per head was £1,828 above the UK average and the highest after Northern Ireland. So the budget deficit is accounted for mainly by higher public expenditure per head rather than lower tax revenue. If public expenditure per head was the average for the UK, Scotland's deficit would be very much smaller and closer to that for the UK.

Why, therefore, is Scotland's public expenditure per head so much above the UK average? Some of this is undoubtedly a consequence of Scotland's geography. Public expenditure has to be much higher in remote areas, of which Scotland has many, to provide the same standard of public service as is available elsewhere. The health service, for example, is much more costly in the Western Isles than in Edinburgh[5] and the same is true of education, where class size in some remote areas is likely to be much smaller. Public expenditure is also higher in areas of deprivation, which is particularly an issue in some of Scotland's urban areas, such as parts of Glasgow, Inverclyde and Lanarkshire. This higher level of public expenditure is why it is often suggested that resources for public expenditure should be based on a needs assessment throughout the regions and nations of the UK.

It is, however, interesting to see how Scotland's higher public expenditure per head compared with the UK average broken down by category of expenditure (Table 3). By far the largest expenditure is for social protection (£26 billion of which the state pension and other support for elderly people comprises 46 per cent) and health (£18 billion) followed by education and training (£9.5 billion). But these are not where the biggest differences from the UK average are. Nothing else exceeds £5 billion except for enterprise and economic development which has increased exceptionally from £1.8 billion in 2019–20 to £11.2 billion in 2020–21 as a result of measures to cope with COVID. But public and common services, housing and community amenity, agriculture, forestry and fishing, environmental protection and transport are where the largest differences are with the UK average.

Table 3: Scottish Public Expenditure by Category in 2020–21

	£ million	£ per head	£ per head UK = 100
General public services			
Public and common services	2,410	440	169
International services	924	16 9	101
Public debt interest	3,861	708	108
Defence	3,637	665	100
Public order and safety	3,392	621	108
Economic affairs			
Enterprise and economic development	11,219[6]	2,052	108
Science and technology	589	107	95
Employment policies	208	38	97
Agriculture forestry and fishing	881	161	169
Transport	4,485	821	122
Environmental protection	1,532	280	149
Housing and community amenity	2,259	413	200
Health	18,026	3,298	101
Recreation, culture and religion	1,571	287	156
Education and training	9,485	1,735	121
Social protection	26,017	4,760	107
EU transactions	278	51	59
Accounting adjustments	8,403	1,537	109
TOTAL	99,176	18,144	111

Note: Expenditure per head calculated on the basis of 5.466 million population for Scotland and 67.081 million for the UK.

Source: 'Government Expenditure and Revenue Scotland 2020–21', ONS UK Population Estimates, National Records of Scotland.

A needs assessment for Scotland was undertaken by the Treasury in the late 1970s but has not been repeated, although the Holtham Commission for Wales argued that a needs assessment would have given Wales a more generous allocation of expenditure.[7] A new needs assessment for Scotland would be a difficult exercise and would be likely to provoke a great deal of dispute about the criteria, since it would be hard to make it truly objective.

But, even if Scotland has some particular needs, it may be true that some services are actually better funded in Scotland than in most other parts of the UK. The Barnett formula, which is presently used to determine levels of expenditure in Scotland and Wales, as the Holtham Commission pointed out, lacks an objective justification. It was expected to be a temporary stopgap arrangement until something better was introduced, at the time of the devolution proposals of the 1970s that never came to fruition. It is no more than an allocation to Scotland of the annual additional expenditure in England on comparable services based on Scotland's population ratio. In Wales, it has resulted in the 'Barnett squeeze' causing expenditure there to move gradually closer to English levels. The same was expected in Scotland but Scotland's higher level of expenditure has proved remarkably durable.

Since this was only introduced as a temporary arrangement, it cannot be expected to last forever and has already been much criticised in England, rightly or wrongly, for giving Scotland too generous an allocation. In the long run, only a system based on need for all the countries and regions of the UK could be properly defended, although it too would be subject to disputes and complaints about how it was calculated.

At the time of the 2014 Scottish referendum, North Sea oil revenues were much greater than now and the optimistic view taken in the 2014 White Paper suggested that they would be large enough to eliminate any fiscal deficit for Scotland.[8] They had fallen from a peak of £11.3 billion in 2011–12 (Scotland's geographical share) and were forecast by the SNP to be still high as the decade progressed. However, the 2011–12 peak was followed by a sharp and unforeseen fall in the price of oil, thereby greatly reducing the value of these revenues. By 2018–19, the oil price had risen from its lowest point but the revenues remained fairly modest at £1.4 billion, only making a small difference to the size of the deficit. By 2020–21, however, the revenues from the North Sea had fallen further to only £550 million (see Chapter 6).

The question for an independent Scotland would be how it should deal with this. The COVID crisis has shown that countries can borrow substantial amounts for an emergency, as the UK also did during the two world wars. A group of economists in the United States, supporters of what they call Modern Monetary Theory (MMT), have argued that deficits do not matter for countries that issue currency because they can always print more and, by issuing bonds, raise money at low interest rates, as has been done with quantitative easing.[9] The only constraint is if the economy gets to the point where inflation rises and starts to be a problem. Payments in the home currency have to be acceptable to debtors, of course. This notion has been subject to a lot of criticism. It may have some validity for the United States because the dollar is widely accepted as an international currency. It might, perhaps, have worked for the UK after the financial crash of 2008–09. Certainly, it makes George Osborne's austerity of the last ten years look as if it was not wholly necessary. But it could not apply to an independent Scotland. If Scotland continued to use the pound or joined the euro, it would not be a currency issuer and would have no ability to print more to pay debt. But, even if it started its own currency, it would have to establish confidence in its management and that would soon evaporate with the country's debtors, if they thought that it was being recklessly issued.

Obviously, therefore, an independent Scotland could not go on indefinitely with a deficit of the present size because, if it did, the markets would lose confidence that the country could avoid default, interest rates would skyrocket and the state would go bankrupt. Unlike the UK, which has no record of default, at least since the Bank of England was created in the seventeenth century, Scotland, as a newly independent state, would have no record of borrowing, so the markets would not have the same confidence that they have in larger, established borrowers. This would mean that interest rates for any borrowing would tend to be higher than for the UK as a whole. There would, therefore, have to be a plan for ensuring that the budget could be brought into balance.

The Sustainable Growth Commission addressed this issue in some detail.[10] It recognised that the Scottish deficit would have to be reduced and the budget brought into balance. But it aimed to avoid austerity such as the UK had after the 2008–09 financial crisis. It argued that public expenditure should be tightly controlled but only so that its rate of increase was less than the growth of GDP. In this way, the budget deficit could gradually reduce, the Commission argued, to around 3 per cent within 5–10 years. Whatever North Sea oil revenues turn out to be, they should be treated as a bonus rather than a means of balancing the budget. The Commission argued that they should be put into a special fund. In a sense, the revenues represent a depletion of natural capital and should not be regarded as normal income.

The consequences of the COVID epidemic have, however, worsened the situation considerably and Brexit will also have an adverse effect, if less domestic and international investment than would otherwise have taken place is a consequence in future years. Even if the economy recovers and is able to return more quickly to where it was before than many people expect, there will be both a UK deficit and a Scottish deficit that are likely to be worse than before and there will be greatly increased debt as well. This would be a serious problem for Scotland that would have to be faced, were it to become independent. It would require resolute and probably unpopular action for some years to come.

The National Debt

Some people of a nationalist persuasion, though not the Scottish government, have argued that the Scottish deficit could be dealt with by cutting the £3,637 million presently shown in the Government Expenditure & Revenue Scotland (GERS) as being allocated to defence and also the £2,347 million that is allocated for payment of interest on the UK national debt, excluding local government fund interest expenditure. These are both shown in the accounts as a population share of the UK total. Defence is covered later but interest on the national debt depends on what share is agreed for Scotland in negotiation.

The national debt has been accumulated by the whole UK and has varied greatly over the years. It rose sharply during the two world wars but declined as a proportion of GDP from a peak of 200 per cent in 1950 to a low point of 32 per cent in the early 2000s. It then rose again following the financial crisis and stood at around 82 per cent of GDP before the COVID outbreak. But the exceptional spending measures taken as a result of COVID to try to safeguard the economy pushed it up to over 100 per cent of GDP again by March 2021. It is likely to go significantly higher before the pandemic is over.

Some of those who argue against an independent Scotland taking its population or GDP share of UK debt say that, if Scotland had been independent during the years of the North Sea oil boom, it would have been able to accumulate substantial surpluses which, in the event, went to the UK Treasury. That may be true, of course. But the fact is that Scotland was not independent at that time. I have argued elsewhere that the UK government should have put the surpluses from the oil revenues into a special fund, as Norway has done.[11] But that was not done either and the surpluses were treated as normal UK government revenue and used to finance ordinary public expenditure for the whole UK. Any attempt to go back on all this would only provoke the UK government to say that Scotland would have been in deficit for many years before North Sea oil was discovered. The oil revenues have, in any case, varied greatly over the years – very large in the early 1980s, much smaller in the 1990s, then recovering up to about 2011–12 before falling to the present low level. This does not seem a productive line of argument and not one that would be accepted in negotiations with the rest of the UK.

The national debt is, of course, in the name of the whole UK with no part of it designated as Scottish, so that it is the UK government that is responsible for it to creditors. But for an independent Scotland to claim that it had no responsibility seems mean and unreasonable. It would only lead to acrimonious relations with the rest of the UK and sour negotiations on other matters. The Sustainable Growth Commission proposed that Scotland should negotiate a balance to be serviced annually and paid by the Scottish government to the UK exchequer, based on a reasonable share of liabilities and assets, as the UK has done in negotiations with the EU. This would require the true value of assets and liabilities to be properly set out and evaluated. This seems reasonable and would presumably end up with Scotland taking responsibility for something approximating to either a population or a GDP share – the latter being very slightly less.

It is important, however, to recognise that the quantitative easing that the Bank of England engaged in, following the financial crisis and again as part of the measures to combat the effects of COVID, has resulted in a large amount of the issued government debt being held by the Bank of England. The Bank at present holds about a third of this debt and it returns the interest payable to the UK Treasury. Assuming this would still be the case at the time of independence, some account should be taken of it in negotiations. Either Scotland's share should be based on UK debt minus what is held by the Bank or the share held by the Bank should be transferred to a Scottish Central Bank when one is set up.

However, assuming Scotland does take a share of the UK national debt, it would be legitimate to argue that it should also have a population or GDP share of the UK reserves of foreign exchange. This would probably be resisted by a UK government but it seems only reasonable, if liabilities are to be divided, that assets must be divided too. A share of the UK foreign exchange reserves would be necessary if the Scottish government wanted to start its own currency. Without such reserves, there would be no means of countering volatile movements in the currency's international value. The prospect of a share of the assets would also be a strong disincentive to a Scottish government thinking of just walking away from negotiating its share of the debt.

Because of the huge amount of borrowing by the UK government (and other governments) as a result of the COVID crisis, the increased burden of debt will, in future, be much higher. Only with time will it be possible to see how matters stand once everything has settled after the COVID crisis. If the UK debt is now (early 2020–21) around 100 per cent of GDP, it will also be very high for Scotland, if it were to take a population or GDP based share, even after allowing for the share of the debt held by the Bank of England. This would result in a difficult situation, especially if interest rates were to rise. Whatever the position, Scotland would need a plan and policy to deal with it. In particular, ways need to be found of increasing the growth of the economy, because only in that way can the deficit and the danger of ever mounting debt be satisfactorily tackled.

The Balance of Payments

Apart from the problem of the budget deficit, there is also the issue of the balance of foreign payments. In the 1960s and 1970s, the UK's balance of payments was seldom out of the news. Problems with the balance of payments were what led to the devaluation in the 1960s and periodic 'stop–go' policies to avoid deficits. This resulted in the UK government's determination to exploit the newly discovered oil resources in the North Sea as quickly as possible, with the expectation of considerable revenues. But, since the move to floating currencies and freedom of capital movements, the balance of payments is seldom mentioned. This is because movements in the currency's exchange rate can take the strain in an age when there are no longer currency controls.

The UK has been running with a deficit on its current account of the balance of payments for many years. Before COVID, this was about 2 per cent of GDP but, earlier, it had been higher – of the order of 4 per cent and one of the highest in the developed world. This is seldom discussed because of a large inflow of foreign money on the capital account. This inflow takes several forms – money coming into institutions in the City of London for investment and various other reasons; foreign companies or individuals buying UK businesses; the takeover of companies, such as Scottish Power, Scottish and Newcastle Breweries, or franchises taken by foreign companies in the railway; investments in North Sea oil and gas; or simply the purchase of property, such as Russian oligarchs or Arabs buying expensive property in London or Highland estates.

There are no official figures for the Scottish balance of payments. Some commentators have pointed out that there are figures showing that Scotland's international exports exceeded imports. But this does not take account of Scotland's trade to and from the rest of the UK, which is greater than the amount going overseas. As Professor David Bell has pointed out,[12] we know that the relative contribution of the trade in goods and services has fallen with the decline of so many industries and employment in these industries has been replaced by activities that are focussed on domestic needs. It is possible to get figures for exports and imports from the Scottish government's input–output tables. These show the supply and use of all goods and services in the Scottish economy and the interdependencies of industries and other activities. The figures for 2017, the latest available year from this source, show exports, excluding North Sea oil and gas, at £84 billion, of which £47.4 billion went to the rest of the UK, £30.5 billion to the rest of the world and £6.2 billion to non-resident households (people living abroad). Imports totalled £94.4 billion, of which £61.9 billion came from the rest of the UK and £32.5 billion from the rest of the world. There is, therefore, a gap or deficit on current account of £10.4 billion or some 7 per cent of Scottish GDP. With the greatly reduced value of oil and gas revenues – £844 million in 2019–2020 and only £550 million in 2020–21[13] – there would still be a substantial deficit when these are included. The effect of the pandemic is only likely to have made this worse.

This shows that Scotland would have a problem with its balance of foreign payments, unless there were substantial inflows on the capital account, and this, coupled with the budget deficit, would force the government to take action. Either the country would have to find a way of boosting GDP so as to be able to increase exports, thereby reducing the deficit on the balance of payments and, at the same time, reducing its budget deficit, or it would be faced with austerity. Reducing labour costs, either by cutting wages or raising productivity to improve the country's competitive position would be one option. But to reduce labour costs is extremely difficult and unpleasant, as some countries in the eurozone have found, and raising productivity would require increased investment.

As an independent country with its own currency, however, there would be pressure to devalue the currency to make the economy more competitive, increase growth and, thereby, with time and adjustment, eliminate both the budget and balance of payments deficits. This is discussed in the next section on currency. But, even then, it would be tricky to manage as it would result in increased prices for imports. It would not work unless any resulting inflationary pressure could be contained so as to get the benefit by increasing the competitiveness of the economy.

The Currency

The Sustainable Growth Commission advocated that an independent Scotland should continue to use sterling after independence, just as Ireland did after 1922. But it would have no role in the management of sterling, no lender of last resort and would be affected by whatever policies the Bank of England thought appropriate for the remainder of the UK. This is what is known as 'sterlingisation', where a country chooses to use the currency of another for convenience and stability. This was not what was proposed at the time of the referendum in 2014, when the Scottish government advocated a full monetary union. But a monetary union will only work if it is agreed by all the participating members, and the UK government of that time made it very clear it would not agree. In any case, as much the smaller member, with an economy only about 8.2 per cent of the UK total, it is not clear how much influence Scotland could expect to have in the management of sterling, even if a monetary union had been agreed.

Mervyn King, the former governor of the Bank of England, has argued that sterlingisation would be perfectly feasible and has pointed out that a number of countries use the dollar on a dollarisation basis.[14] He, therefore, considered that this would be the right policy for an independent Scotland to follow. That was, however, before the EU referendum and the decision of the UK to leave the EU, which is likely to adversely affect the Scottish economy. It would not be sensible to break the link with sterling immediately on independence, as Scotland would not have the infrastructure to manage its own currency nor, unless there was agreement with the remainder of the UK, a share of the reserves of foreign currency. The

Sustainable Growth Commission advocated the setting up of a Scottish central bank but it would take time do this.

Professor Ronald MacDonald of the Adam Smith Business School at the University of Glasgow, an acknowledged expert in international finance, rejects the sterlingisation proposal on the grounds that, with twin deficits both on the budget and the current account of the balance of payments, it would not replace the sharing of risk that Scotland has as part of the UK.[15] In the short term, even if taxes were raised or public expenditure cut, Scotland would have to borrow to finance both of these deficits. UK borrowing is presently extremely cheap and, therefore, attractive but, as a new borrower with no long record of credibility like the UK, Scotland would have to pay significantly more on its borrowing and, if lenders thought there was any danger of default, the cost could become excessive so that it could not be sustained. Interest rates would be in danger of constantly increasing in a vicious circle, resulting in eventual collapse. This is not unlike the position of Greece as a member of the eurozone in recent years. If Scotland was forced to leave sterling by pressure of the markets – rather as the currency union between the Czech Republic and Slovakia broke up – its new currency would come in at a lower rate, amounting to a forced devaluation. But the borrowing that had been done in sterling would then still be a problem, as it would have to be repaid in sterling unless it could be re-designated in Scottish currency. This is not unprecedented – the members of the eurozone re-designated their national debts in euros. But this would obviously be resisted by the rest of the UK as, in sterling terms, it would amount to a reduction in what was paid. Depending on what happened to exchange rates, therefore, repayment in sterling could result in a currency crisis.

Provided this debt issue can be resolved, it would make sense to establish a Scottish currency as soon as the necessary infrastructure of a Scottish Central Bank could be established. The value of the currency could then adjust to reflect the needs of the economy properly. This could be important both for Scotland's budget deficit and its balance of payments by making the economy more competitive and, thereby, improving its rate of economic growth. But it would be tricky and would require careful management because, if there was expectation that this was to be the policy, it would result in speculation immediately after independence. There could be a sudden movement of funds to the safety of the UK, forcing a break of the link with sterling, as happened when the Czech and Slovak republics separated. It would then become very hard to borrow and costly to do so, at least until the new currency was in place and had had time to settle. This would make life very difficult and potentially damaging to Scottish financial institutions that are a very important part of the economy.

There is a strong case that the strength of the financial sector in London and the amount of money being invested there from abroad have resulted in an exchange rate that has been too high for the rest of the UK economy. With its own currency, Scotland could avoid this, allowing its currency to reflect the proper strength of the economy. It should be noted, however, that the effect of North Sea oil is important here. If Scotland had had its own currency in the early 1980s or at any time when the revenues from oil were really substantial, there would have been pressure for the exchange rate to rise, causing serious damage to the rest of the economy – what is sometimes called the 'resource curse'. Faced with this, the Norwegian government has invested much of its oil fund abroad with the outflow of capital invested helping to keep the exchange rate down. Scotland would be unlikely to be affected by this now that the oil revenues are greatly reduced which, ironically, would make the management of an exchange rate easier.

Once a Scottish currency was established at a rate that made the economy competitive, the right policy, in my view, would then be to peg it to either the pound or the euro, as the Danish government has pegged the krone to the euro.

This would help to avoid the destabilising fluctuations that affected the Irish punt, when it was freely floating after the peg with sterling was removed in the late 1970s, and would be liable to affect the currency of any small country.

I would not advocate adopting the euro and joining the eurozone. If Scotland decided to apply for full membership of the EU, it would probably be expected to accept this as an ultimate objective. But the requirements of monetary union have very adversely affected several countries, notably in southern Europe and in particular Greece (see Chapter 10). This is inevitable if a member state in a currency union cannot keep inflation in sufficient check to maintain the competitive position of its economy against other members of the union.

As discussed earlier, even countries in the EU that do not have a formally agreed opt-out cannot be forced to join. Although countries that join the EU have to accept that joining the euro is one of the aims, there is an intermediate stage after joining the EU and participating fully in the single market when countries are expected to gradually integrate their monetary policy with the EU and participate in the exchange rate mechanism.[16] At the present, eight of the 27 EU countries have not joined the eurozone and most of them look unlikely to do so any time soon. Scotland's present budget deficit would, in any case, mean that it did not meet the requirements to join the eurozone and it could decide later to hold a referendum on the issue, as Sweden did.

If Scotland was a member of the European Economic Area rather than a full member of the EU, as discussed earlier, membership of the eurozone would not be necessary, even as an ultimate objective. So long as a country has its own currency, even if it is pegged to the pound or the euro, its debt would be in national currency and it could, *in extremis*, remove the peg to alter its exchange rate if that were necessary to make its economy competitive. Having its own currency gives a country a degree of economic sovereignty that could prove to be very important. Membership of the euro made conditions exceptionally bad in Greece when it was in crisis and, because its debt was in euros and many European banks of other countries were creditors, it was very difficult to leave.[17]

Other Assets to be Divided

Scotland would, of course, have to make its own defence arrangements and decide how much it should spend, whether it would join NATO, whether the present UK defence forces should be split and, if so, how that would be done. Several NATO countries have been severely criticised by the United States for depending too much on US support and not spending the 2 per cent of GDP on defence which is the amount set as a target at the Wales Summit of NATO held in Cardiff in 2014. With Russia in a more bellicose mood and penetrating UK airspace, including Scottish airspace, from time to time and relations with China worsening, it hardly seems the right moment to be cutting defence expenditure.

Dividing the armed forces between Scotland and the remainder of the UK following independence would be one of the more difficult decisions involved in splitting UK assets. Most likely Scotland would simply have to start from scratch, despite the large amount of Scottish personnel presently in UK armed forces, and decide what expenditure it should provide and what armed forces it should have. The nuclear base on the Clyde is a particular problem. Would it have to go, as the SNP insist, or would some arrangement be found for it to stay at least until the rest of the UK made some other arrangement, with perhaps financial compensation in the meantime? In exchange for the UK keeping the base, the Scottish government might demand a substantial rent, which would still be cheaper for the rest of the UK than having to build a new base elsewhere.

The Govan and Scotstoun shipyards on the Clyde, as well as Rosyth, are dependent on orders from the UK for naval ships. This could not be expected to continue as the UK has never ordered ships for its forces except from domestic shipyards. This loss of economic activity would potentially be serious and, if the Scottish government was ordering ships for its own newly formed navy, to what extent would this compensate for the loss of UK business?

Other assets, such as UK government departments in Scotland, the BBC, the Crown Estate, Network Rail, Royal Mail and the Meteorological Office come immediately to mind. The UK's foreign exchange reserves were mentioned earlier but there would be many others. These would mostly be easier than defence but all this would have to be faced. Either they would have to be divided or paid for to the rest of the UK on some kind of agency basis.

4

Other challenges for a
Scottish government

All of the previous points show that the government of an independent Scotland would have to face some formidable issues that would be both important and difficult to deal with. But there are other matters which will press hard on the budget of a newly independent state, some of which are dealt with in this chapter. The present Scottish government, understandably, has had its hands full with the pandemic and Scottish voters may not want to face further major problems for some considerable time but, apart from the successful rollout of the COVID vaccine, the Westminster government is not becoming any more popular in Scotland and Brexit is unlikely to help. So, if the issue of the constitution returns with a referendum, all these issues will need to be faced.

The First Minister, Nicola Sturgeon, is by any standard an able and impressive politician but, in the view of many commentators, the government has a mixed record. Apart from dealing with the issues in the last section, there are other matters where there will be a demand for funding that would need to be faced. Health and education are the two areas of the Scottish government's present responsibility that cost the most in the Scottish budget, although social protection, which is at present mainly the responsibility of the UK government, costs substantially more. All of these are going to result in a demand for more resources, if public hopes and expectations are to be met.

Health

The continually increasing cost of healthcare is likely to give rise to one of the biggest demands on the finances of the government of an independent Scotland. Thanks to an ever-growing proportion of elderly people in our society, many kept alive by remarkable advances in medical science, the cost of healthcare has been rising and will continue to rise faster than the growth of the country's GDP. This is a major problem for all countries. In 2020–21, the cost of health in Scotland's budget was £18.8 billion. But it is widely accepted that the NHS has had insufficient funding for some years past and the COVID crisis has shown this up. Over the last 20 years or so, the UK government has attempted to meet increasing health costs by cutting back on other services, such as defence, social care, welfare and infrastructure spending, but that cannot continue.

Most European countries finance their health services through an insurance system with people able to reclaim the cost of visiting a GP and hospital treatment. In Ireland, for example, there is a fee for visiting a GP. But the pressures are the same in all countries and, while in some countries there appears to be greater provision, all face the same problems. The UK spends a lower proportion of its GDP on healthcare than comparable countries, such as France or Germany, and much less than the United States although, there, a sizeable proportion of the population is not covered by insurance at all. It can be claimed that, for what it spends, the UK gets a very good service. But it is not enough. Staff work very hard, in many cases for moderate pay, and there is a large number of vacancies both for nurses and doctors, resulting in many being recruited from other countries.

If Scotland becomes independent, the government will have to consider how best to meet this continuing challenge and how to pay for it. Should it, for example, make greater use of an insurance system like France or Germany? But a change in system is unlikely to make much difference to the demands on the taxpayer and charging fees, even if reclaimable, would probably be anathema to the public who are used to a totally free service. Scotland has a proud history of its medical schools and the modern NHS is greatly valued by the population. Arguably Scotland's NHS has been slightly better funded over the years than in England but the figures in Table 3 in the previous chapter show that the difference is negligible now. The service badly needs more resources, as it does elsewhere in the UK.

Over the last few years, several new hospitals have been built, such as the new Royal Infirmary of Edinburgh and the Queen Elizabeth University Hospital (QEUH) in Glasgow. Ministers have been much criticised for the long delay over the opening of the new Royal Hospital for Children and Young People which replaced the Sick Kids' Hospital in Edinburgh, due to inadequacies of the ventilation system. This and the similar problems at the new QEUH are serious and should not have happened but they arise from defects that are a matter between the architects, the construction company and the Health Board as commissioning body. They should not be continuing problems.

Looking to the future, what matters is the expected escalating cost of healthcare as a result of the changing demography – an increasingly ageing population and a decreasing working population with income to pay for it – combined with advances in medical science. These would be a problem for the budget of the newly independent Scotland and Ministers will have to be aware of this and plan how they are going to cope with it.

Care of the Elderly

Related to this are the problems over the provision of care for the elderly. In the 1970s, an elderly relative who needed care in an institution could be accommodated in a hospital where, as at the City Hospital in Edinburgh, there were wards specifically for the elderly. Alternatively there were private care homes but, inevitably, these were costly. In the 1980s, the UK government closed almost all the NHS hospital accommodation for the elderly and a decision was taken that meant those who no longer needed medical intervention but needed care should be catered for either by care services at home or in private care homes. For those unable to meet the cost, local authorities had to provide the funds. But, over these years, as the population has aged, the number of the elderly needing care has increased enormously.

In Scotland the coalition government in 2002 passed legislation with cross-party support to provide free personal and nursing care for the elderly. This was extended later to those under 65 who needed it and it was not only for those in care homes but also for those needing care at home. Contrary to a common misperception, especially in England, this does not cover all the costs of a care home, only about half, because the so called 'hotel costs' of accommodation and meals were still charged, subject to a means test. Local authorities were only required to pay for those who the means test showed could not pay for their care themselves.

The Scottish government has set up new Integration Joint Boards (IJBs) thus bringing together local authority social care and NHS services with a budget drawn from existing local authority and NHS budgets. The intention is that they would deliver more efficient health and social care services. However, although this demonstrates the government's concern with the situation, there are still problems and the then Auditor General for Scotland, Caroline Gardner, described the progress made by these integrated authorities as slow.

In November 2020, the government announced a major review to look at every aspect of social care in Scotland chaired by Derek Feeley, a former Director General for Health and Social Care and Chief Executive of NHS Scotland, with an advisory panel combining Scottish and international experts. The report of this review was published in February 2021 and has far reaching recommendations.[1] It recommends that a National Care Service (NCS) be set up and that it should have similar standing to the National Health Service. Accountability for social care should be transferred from local authorities directly to the Scottish government with a specified Minister given responsibility. The NCS would set standards and presumably be responsible for ensuring overall funding. The Feeley Report does not go as far as recommending that care homes be taken into the public sector, where they would be controlled and regulated as hospitals are. If accountability is going to rest with the NCS and Scottish Ministers, however, that would go a long way towards ensuring standards. It would also ensure closer cooperation between the care sector and the NHS.

There is continuing concern over funding of the sector and this is a problem for the Scottish government. Because of the cost, the recommendations would be difficult to implement at present, unless major reform in England also results in more money being available for Scotland through the Barnett formula. The report, of course, deals with all social care both in care homes and at home and concludes that fewer people are receiving care than would be expected to need it and that this gap needs to be covered. It recognises that there is a need for investment in care facilities. Many of those who work in the sector are poorly paid and the report recommends increasing the real living wage to £9.50 an hour. This would be paid to all staff in adult care support, including those working in care homes, home care, housing support, day care and adult placement services The cost of implementing the real living wage represents a floor and pay rates might well be above this. It is recognised that a career in care services needs to be properly recognised and valued. It should be accorded a proper status.

The report's recommendations would mean that all social care would be free at the point of need, since personal and nursing care are already free in Scotland, and that the only remaining cost would be for accommodation, whether at home or in a care home. These costs would generally be higher for those living in care homes than for those receiving care at home but the reports says that, since a person's income would generally pay for accommodation at home, the same should apply to the accommodation cost of a care home. If the person's income is insufficient, the balance would be funded by the local authority, subject to a means test. The report takes the view that it is reasonable for a person's income to be subject to a charge because the person would otherwise be paying for their own accommodation. They did not consider whether the means test presently applied was appropriate but did say that this could, in future, be considered by the NCS.

Throughout the whole of the UK, the situation over care homes is critical and this came increasingly to public attention during the COVID pandemic. The care sector is expensive but investment in more facilities is needed and the sector is clearly underfunded throughout the UK. While many homes are good, improvements are needed and there have been scandals over the quality of care some homes have provided. People who work in the sector are poorly paid, often getting no more than the minimum wage, and care homes frequently rely on workers recruited from abroad who, as a result of Brexit, may be less available in future. Some care homes are finding it difficult to remain solvent as their operations are increasingly – and quite rightly – regulated not only on staffing levels and qualifications but also on building standards. Those residents who can afford to pay are increasingly finding that they are actually having to pay more than those funded by local authorities, whom they are in effect subsidising.

A serious consequence is the prevalence of bed blocking in acute hospitals. Hospitals often find that patients, for whom they can no longer provide useful medical intervention, are difficult to discharge, if they are not fit enough to go home or cannot be looked after at home. A bed in a care home may not be available; the person needing care may be reluctant or unable to meet the cost; or a local authority may not be able to find the necessary funding. But, despite personal and nursing care being free in Scotland, these problems still remain and, during the COVID crisis, there was a more urgent need to remove bed blockers from acute hospitals which resulted in many of them being transferred to care homes. This has been blamed as one of the causes of the high incidence of COVID in these homes. This situation has remained unresolved for many years.

It is not only unsatisfactory to have bed blocking in acute hospitals, where the space is needed for other patients, but it is also extremely expensive – a bed in an acute hospital, with the associated care, costs more than a bed in an expensive hotel. The policy, so far, of relying on private care homes can, therefore, only be described as a serious failure. Edinburgh, for example, used to have wards in the City Hospital and several small hospitals where patients could be moved from the acute wards in large hospitals. All of these have been closed and, for the sake of the elderly, one wishes they were still there. The same situation applies in other cities and towns in Scotland. The recommendations of the Feeley Report, if implemented, would go a long way to remedy this and hopefully end the problem of bed blocking in hospitals.

There has been much concern about the cost to individuals which, under the present arrangements, can involve running down their own funds to £23,250 to pay costs. The Conservative government set up the Dilnot Commission in 2010 and it issued a comprehensive report a year later. But successive governments have failed to implement its recommendations, probably because any solution is expensive. This is not really tackled in the Feeley Report, which simply says that it is considered reasonable for those in care homes to contribute to the accommodation costs, as they would be doing this if they were at home. It is recognised, however, that the cost of accommodation in a care home is likely to be higher than the cost of accommodation at home. A solution would need to be found to this by an independent Scotland's government if it has not been dealt with before independence.

The Dilnot Commission stopped short of advocating that the full cost of care homes should be taken into the public sector. But it recommended that there should be a cap on the cost anyone should pay for care in their lifetime: they set this at £35,000, no matter what a person's means may be. It should be possible, the Commission said, for people to take out insurance to cover this cost, if they did not want to risk having to meet it themselves. The Commission also recommended that the present level of £23,250 to which a person's assets, however large, are run down to cover the cost of care should be raised to £100,000. People in residential care, however, should pay a nationally fixed sum towards living costs, which it was expected would be affordable from their income from the state pension. Although these recommendations would cost a significant amount, they offered a sensible way forward and the Commission estimated that two thirds of people over 65 would have care needs of less than £35,000. These costs of course were estimates at the time of the Dilnot report, which was ten years ago. They will be substantially higher now. Moreover, the proposals dealt only with the costs falling on individuals; they did not cover estimated investment needed or improved pay for staff. It was no doubt because of the high cost involved, which would have had implications for taxation, that no action was taken to implement the proposals.

However, the present UK government promised during the election in 2019 to 'fix once and for all' the crisis in social care, and in September 2021, as this book was already in process of publication, plans were announced that were intended to honour this pledge. An additional £12 billion for health and social care is to be made available across the UK. This is intended to tackle the backlog built up in the NHS because of the COVID pandemic and to address the urgent need for improvement and reform in social care that successive governments had failed to deal with.

These changes are to be paid for by an increase in National Insurance of 1.25 per cent, which would be ring-fenced so that it became a dedicated levy, an increase in the tax on dividend payments and suspension for one year of the triple lock on pension increases. It is expected that the bulk of this substantial increase in funding will be needed by the NHS to clear the backlog as a result of the pandemic, and some scepticism has been expressed about the amount that would be available for social care. The tax increases will apply to Scotland as elsewhere in the UK and there will also be UK-wide changes to payments for care for which individuals are responsible. From October 2023 there is to be a cap of £86,000 on the amount that anyone would have to pay for care and in future no one would be required to pay at all if their assets were less than £20,000. Above that a taper would result in only those with assets over £100,000 meeting the full cost. The Scottish share of the funding will be determined by the Barnett formula and will probably be around £1 billion. It will then be for the Scottish Government to allocate. Kate Forbes, the finance minister, has said that in common with previous practice it will all be passed on to be spent on health and social care. At the time of writing no details of this are available. Much will presumably go to the NHS, but the remainder would be available for improvements in social care. Consultation is now in progress on the proposed National Care Service and it remains to be seen how it might be affected by this increased funding.

The Feeley Report estimated that its recommendations would cost £660 million or about 0.4 per cent of Scotland's GDP. This is a huge cost, as the report recognises, but it may now be possible to meet at least part of this from the consequential funds for Scotland of this latest announcement. The Feeley Report had outlined various ways in which the cost of its proposals might be met, such as the introduction of mandatory social insurance, a new local tax, changes to devolved taxes or the devolution of some reserved taxes. But these may not be necessary if sufficient funding comes from the UK-wide changes. Much will therefore depend on what eventually happens in the UK. Because the Scottish Government already meets the cost of personal care and nursing care, leaving only the accommodation costs and the costs of improving pay and facilities, it should be possible for major improvements to be made. But a lot will depend on how much of the additional funds are required to meet the backlog problems in the NHS. A complete solution will still be expensive but if independence happens, it would be one of the major challenges facing the government of the newly independent country.

Education

(1) Schools

Nicola Sturgeon has said that education, for which the Scottish government paid £9.5 billion in 2020–21, is one of her greatest priorities but, so far, the results have not been impressive and Scotland has slipped down the Organisation for Economic Cooperation and Development's Programme for International Student Assessment (OECD's PISA) tables. While many pupils do well and end up with good qualifications, too many end up with poor literary and numeracy skills, which fit them only for low-skilled jobs or unemployment. There is also a serious gap between the results achieved in better-off areas and those in areas of deprivation and this may well have worsened during the COVID lockdowns. Improving this attainment gap is certainly not easy and will probably require more resources. Scottish pupils must have a good foundation of literacy and numeracy if they are to build their skills in sciences, languages, medicine, social sciences and engineering. Perhaps the Scottish government needs to be prepared to be more radical in pushing changes, if these things are to be achieved. The economy in future will require more skilled labour, often with professional qualifications, and the expectation is that there will be less opportunity for the unskilled.

If Scotland is going to attach importance to its relationship with Europe, more attention should also be devoted to learning foreign languages. Since joining the then EEC in 1973, one might have expected that more emphasis would have been put on European languages in school but the reverse seems to have been the case. It is not satisfactory to rely on people from other countries being able to speak English – as increasingly many of them do – because it is becoming an international language. For any contact, whether negotiating in business or dealing with tourists, it is an advantage to be able to understand the language of those with whom one is dealing. That seems to have been taken to heart in other European countries but not in the UK. The proficiency in languages across Europe only shows that learning to speak a foreign language does not in any way adversely affect ability to cope with other subjects at school.

Perhaps the time has come for a major reappraisal of school education, as Jack McConnell, a former First Minister and Education Minister and himself a former teacher, has argued.[2] He says there should be no more clarification of Curriculum for Excellence, which has made matters worse. Instead, acquiring knowledge, proof of attainment and freedom for schools to innovate should be at the core of the system. Curriculum for Excellence was introduced in 2010, following consultation and a review in 2003 by the then coalition government. But, rightly or wrongly, it has been a source of complaint from many teachers and parents. It is not so much a curriculum as a set of fairly vague educational ideas and aspirations and many would argue that it is not working. Many school pupils are not doing as well as their predecessors used to do or as their counterparts in schools abroad.

As Lord McConnell says, the acquisition of knowledge should be central to our education and there needs to be a proper system of attainment. In this respect, the cancelation of exams because of the COVID pandemic was most unfortunate even if it was unavoidable. As a result of strong pressure from teachers' unions and opposition parties, the government announced in December 2020 its decision also to cancel Highers and Advanced Highers in 2021.[3] The Welsh government cancelled exams in Wales too.

When the exams were cancelled in 2020, in England as well as Scotland, teachers' assessments were used to grade pupils instead but the Scottish Qualifications Agency at first applied an algorithm, which was intended to standardise the results by adjusting the teachers' assessments to how their schools had performed in previous years. This caused a major row and had to be abandoned in England as well as Scotland. But the result has been that a larger proportion of pupils have been given high marks and universities have had to admit many more applicants than would have been normal. As a result, at St Andrews University some students have had to be accommodated in Dundee for lack of space in St Andrews. There have been claims that the attainment gap between schools in deprived areas and those in wealthier areas has been reduced. Is this real or a result of the assessment system used? The impression one gets is that the effect of the COVID lockdowns may well have increased the gap, as some pupils in deprived areas may be less likely to have received help and supervision from parents than those in wealthier areas. One also hears that independent schools have done much more for their pupils in providing work and instruction than many state schools. There can be no good reason for this. The closing of this attainment gap is most important but it needs to be closed properly. This requires targeted action but not at the expense of those in better-off areas.

For all these reasons, it is greatly to be regretted that the results of exams again depended on teachers' assessments, although these were backed up by course work and not adjusted by the algorithm, as was the case in 2020. After being off school for a long time, many pupils had to face tests within the first few days of their return – which amounted, in some people's view, to exams by another name. All of this gives the impression that the situation was not properly thought through and that decisions were taken in haste.

According to the press, John Swinney, the Cabinet Secretary for Education, confirmed that he is considering proposals to scrap exams permanently. In my view, this would be a serious error. An objective assessment of pupils' performances is certainly necessary and, whatever the short-comings of any exam system – and there are several – no better way of doing it has ever been found. The government is rightly anxious to close the attainment gap, but that will also lead to pressure on teachers, if assessments depend on them, to upgrade marks, especially in poorer areas. Moreover, teachers' assessments will tend to be seen as reflecting on the ability of the teacher as well as pupils and there will always be pressure to show results as favourably as possible. To rely on them, however adjusted, is not a satisfactory alternative and is unlikely to be considered as such by either employers or universities. If school exams were to be abolished, entry exams for university might in the end have to be introduced. It is greatly to be hoped, therefore, that, once the pandemic has passed, schools get back to a properly designed exam system.

It is regrettable too that the government's Schools Inspectorate is no longer the independent entity it once was when assessing standards was its main function. Now part of Education Scotland, an executive agency of government directly responsible to the Cabinet Secretary for Education, it is charged with ensuring government policy is implemented rather than providing an independent assessment of standards. It, therefore, no longer has the status it once had.

The morale of teachers is crucial and it was better after the review that I led in 2000 resulted in higher pay and some important other changes.[4] But the situation needs to be looked at again. The scheme for chartered teachers has been dropped partly, it would seem, because local authorities with pressure on funds did not want to employ a more expensive chartered teacher if a cheaper non-chartered one was available. That is regrettable. Chartered status should never have depended only on the acquiring of paper qualifications but on proper assessment of the ability of teachers to teach because such ability varies, as everyone knows. This has long been resisted by the teachers' unions but such assessments are vital to improvement.

It is also important to avoid constantly changing the system. That is one of the complaints over Curriculum for Excellence, but was also a complaint for many years before that. One of the most constant complaints from schools was about never-ending government interference. Once priorities in education are decided and a satisfactory system put in place, the government should not try to micromanage school education, as it has done too often in the past. At one time, Scotland had a school education system that was superior to other parts of the UK and envied by other countries. That is not the position now but it should be an ambition to get back to that with whatever action is necessary. It will require a willingness to confront any vested interest that tries to impede reform.

(2) Universities

Scotland has a deservedly high reputation for its universities but they have become financially dependent on a large number of foreign students, many of whom are now from China. Since the decision was taken not to charge fees to Scottish students, it was an EU requirement that this automatically applied also to students from other EU member countries. The Scottish government then paid the fees for Scottish students but could not afford to pay as much as some other students paid. The EU rule did not apply to differences within a member state and so students from England, Wales and Northern Ireland (but not the Republic of Ireland) are liable to pay up to £9,000 a year. Students from outside the EU may have to pay even more. This is a shambles. It has resulted in distorting the whole student intake. A cap had to be put on the number of Scottish students the universities could admit because the universities had, for financial reasons, to admit as many fee-paying students as possible, if they were to be financially viable.

As a result of EU membership, the UK was able to participate in the Erasmus student exchange programme, enabling students to study in EU countries other than their own. This has been of great benefit in widening the horizons of those who took part and over three million students have participated since the scheme was started. The UK could have continued its membership after Brexit but chose not to do so and it has been announced that it will start the new Turing Scheme for UK students instead. It is not clear yet how this will work but it is suspected that it will be less expensive and may, therefore, be a somewhat weaker scheme. If so, that is a pity as UK and Scottish students have certainly benefited from the Erasmus Programme. It is interesting that the Welsh government have announced that they wish to continue the Erasmus programme as it considers it much better than the UK's replacement.

Apart from research, the primary function of the Scottish universities, as Alexander McCall Smith has so clearly argued, should be to educate students from Scotland.[5] One hears, for example, that it is difficult for Scottish school leavers to get a place to study medicine at a Scottish university and this at a time when there is a serious shortage of doctors in Scotland. The result is that the NHS is dependent on a significant number of doctors from the EU and further afield. This cannot be right. If school leavers meet the necessary standards for university entry, they should be able to get a place. Like much else, a solution will be expensive but, if Scotland becomes independent, the government would have to deal with it.

(3) Vocational Skills

One of the most serious weaknesses in the whole UK is that many vocational skills have been traditionally regarded as of less importance than academic studies at university. One consequence of this was that many technical colleges – especially what were called in Scotland the 'Central Institutions', funded directly by central government – aspired to become universities, leading in Scotland to a substantial increase in their number. The last Labour government was aiming for 50 per cent of school leavers to go to university and, in Scotland, it is now close to that figure. It was undoubtedly right to increase the availability of university education to many more school leavers. But the number of colleges of further education with vocational courses was reduced with amalgamations, probably to help the Scottish government to pay for its policy of abolishing fees for Scottish and EU university students.

In many European countries school pupils have a choice of either going on to study vocational subjects with the aim of taking an apprenticeship and qualifying at a college or taking more academic studies leading to university entry. The implication is that all young people should do one or the other. Not everyone is suited to or wants further academic work but they may be able to develop useful practical skills. For very many years, there have been complaints about the shortage of skilled workers in the UK and a consequence was the large number that came from Europe after the former communist countries joined the EU. They made a useful contribution to the UK economy but remedying this shortage of skills in the UK labour force should be a priority. If the Scottish economy is to achieve the sort of growth it would need after independence, this is of major importance. The introduction of modern apprenticeships in Scotland was a valuable innovation and is the right way forward to increase skills. The modern age requires more rather than less skilled labour and steps to achieve this need to be given priority.

Social Protection

At £26 billion in 2020–21, more money is spent on social

protection than on health and education combined and by far the greatest part of it – £17.1 billion – is spent by the UK government. This includes the state pension, which comprises over 40 per cent of the total. The Scottish government is responsible for £8.9 billion, which includes the Scottish Welfare Fund, the Council Tax Reduction Scheme and spending on Discretionary Housing Benefits. All of these are administered by local authorities. This figure also now includes several recently devolved social security allowances – Disability Living Allowance and Personal Independence Payment which, together, make up £2.1 billion, Carer's Allowance, Attendance Allowance, Winter Fuel Payment and a number of smaller items. These additional items have virtually doubled the amount for which the Scottish government was previously responsible.

If Scotland becomes independent, all expenditure on social protection would, of course, become the responsibility of the Scottish government. This would be a big change and a huge increase in the Scottish government's role. It would then be for Scottish Ministers to decide on their priorities. The 40 per cent or so spent on the state pension presumably would not change but the rest could either be increased or reduced depending on the government's policies, the performance of the economy and the need to support those in need. The more unemployment or social distress, the higher would be the claims on social protection while, if unemployment was low and the economy prospering, the amount of support required would be lower. This is, of course, very hard to predict for a newly independent country. But it could make a big difference to the overall Scottish budget balance – just as revenue would also depend on the economy's performance.

It is this part of the social protection expenditure – excluding the state pension – that would be most subject to demands for an increase. The move from the previous wide range of benefits to Universal Credit, while a sensible rationalisation, was done in a way that involved a significant cut. There are also complaints about the delay involved for those who apply. The COVID pandemic has made the inadequacies of this clear. If people lose their jobs as a result of government action, they should be able to get enough support to avoid the kind of severe poverty that is threatening many people. The furlough scheme protected many jobs but those who did not qualify had no recourse other than to Universal Credit. There will undoubtedly be pressure on the government of an independent Scotland to make Universal Credit, or whatever replaces it, more generous.

A number of people have been pressing for a new scheme of 'Universal Basic Income' which would be paid to everyone, not only to those who are claiming benefits. It would obviously involve increased taxation, even if it was introduced at quite a modest level, but, if it was introduced at a level that would avoid poverty, including for those previously dependent on benefits, the cost would be very high indeed. This does not seem to be practical for an independent Scotland.

But it is a serious concern that a substantial portion of welfare payments go to those in work but receiving inadequate pay. Maybe this points to a need to raise the minimum wage but that could result in many of these poorly paid jobs simply being lost altogether. If Scotland was prosperous enough, with significant employment opportunities, that might not matter. It is one of the features of the modern economy that hollowing out of previously good jobs with globalisation has meant that there are not enough employment opportunities with decently paid work. A comprehensive review of the benefit system, therefore, does seem to be something that is needed and which the government would be pressed to undertake.

Unfortunately, increased expenditure on social protection, added to what would be pressed for on education and health, would only add to the difficulties for the government of a newly independent state trying to cope with securing something like balance in its budget.

The economy

The Scottish economy has been completely transformed over the last half a century or so. It has been a difficult time, punctuated by many disappointments but also by opportunities. In the 1960s, employment in manufacturing amounted to over 30 per cent of the workforce and contributed 36 per cent of GDP.[1] Today, manufacturing contributes only just over 10 per cent of GDP and employment. There is no more than a toehold in shipbuilding, steel and textiles and no deep-coal mining, the industries that were pre-eminent in the 1960s. This is a reduction that earlier generations would have found hard to believe.

Most of the heavy engineering has also gone. And many of the companies from abroad that settled in Scotland have also gone. The success in the 1980s in attracting the electronics industry, at one time thought to be a replacement for the heavy industry that had been lost, has also ended in disappointment. Too much of what came were assembly plants which with globalisation have migrated to countries where labour is cheaper.

In view of all this, it is remarkable that, in recent years, before the COVID pandemic, unemployment rates in Scotland were low, generally a little lower than or equal to the UK average. This compares with the 1960s, when Scottish unemployment was also low but generally about twice the UK average. And, in place of heavy emigration which, in the

1960s, was equivalent to the whole population of Edinburgh – with roughly equal numbers going to the rest of the UK and overseas destinations – there has been small net immigration. In the 1950s and 1960s, Scotland's GDP per head was one of the lowest in the UK, along with Wales and Northern Ireland. Now, it is exceeded only by London, the South-East and the Eastern Region of England. Although Scotland's rate of economic growth has generally been below that of the UK, it has been matched by a lower population growth.

In the circumstances, it is surprising that the Scottish economy has done so well. The discovery and then development of North Sea oil and gas has, of course, given the economy a major boost, creating employment opportunities especially in the north-east. But the fall in the oil price since the 2014 referendum, coupled with the fact that much of the resource has now been exploited and concern about the effect of fossil fuels on the environment, means that it cannot be expected to contribute as much growth in future.

It is not realistic to think of getting back to the kind of economy that Scotland had in the past. Everything has moved on and circumstances have changed. Decline in the older industries was inevitable and all that could have been hoped for was that it would have happened more gradually. Some businesses that might have been saved were lost. But the decline of manufacturing continued through the 1980s and 1990s into the present century. This is similar to but not unlike what has happened in all the advanced European countries although, in the UK, it was particularly marked and, in Scotland, even more so.

Some of the decline in manufacturing, especially when it was very rapid in the early 1980s, seemed to me far too brutal, more than necessary and mainly caused by the combination of the UK's extreme monetarist economic policies and the growth in North Sea oil output, with its large inflow of revenues to government. Both of these pushed the sterling exchange rate up from $1.60 to the pound in the late

1970s to \$2.40 in the early 1980s. Nothing was done to try to counteract these effects and, at this exchange rate, it was very difficult even for very efficient firms, not just those in the older industries, to compete internationally.

It has left Scotland with an economy that is based mainly on services. The growth of financial and business services has been particularly important, as have tourism and services related to health and social work. As Professor David Bell has pointed out, this has resulted in an economy where the focus of production has changed from markets outside Scotland to domestic consumption and where exports are exceeded by imports, as was explained in Chapter 3.[2] In the long run, this would not be sustainable for an independent country. It is, therefore, of major importance to strengthen the economy's export performance, not only in manufacturing but including, of course, services, such as tourism and finance, which can have substantial foreign earnings.

As is also explained in Chapter 3, in order to improve competitiveness in international markets and encourage investment to increase productivity, either labour costs have to be reduced in a fixed currency regime – if Scotland retains sterling as its currency – or – if it has its own currency – its exchange rate against other currencies needs to be allowed to settle at a level that makes the economy competitive. Neither of these would be easy. Forcing labour costs down is both difficult and unpleasant but introducing a new currency, while probably preferable, introduces all sorts of risks not only internationally but also to domestic business and consumers, who would face more expensive imported products. It could cause some financial businesses to relocate, even if it encouraged others to settle in Scotland to get the advantage of a more competitive exchange rate. It also carries the implication that, if the exchange rate falls to make the economy more able to compete internationally, this will result in imported goods being more expensive and, therefore, result in inflation.

Are there perhaps ways of stimulating the economy

without incurring either of these problems? Ways have to be found to improve productivity and that requires investment either in new enterprises or improving the performance of existing firms. The Scottish economy already has policies and infrastructure to tackle this. Financial assistance is still available to help firms start up and expand their operations. The experience of the last half century was that the economy was not able to generate sufficient growth domestically to maintain full employment, even with such measures, when faced with the huge loss of jobs in the older traditional industries.

Major efforts were, therefore, made to attract investment from abroad. In this Scotland was and still is at the present time very successful, attracting more foreign investment than any part of the UK outside London, but whether that will continue after Brexit has its full effect must be open to question. Indeed the longer-term consequences of Brexit on investment, particularly from overseas but also from domestic sources, are probably more serious for the Scottish economy than the shorter-term dislocation, serious though that is also likely to be. It is extremely disappointing that the success in the 1980s in attracting the electronics industry did not lead to more lasting benefit. But globalisation has meant that firms can locate anywhere in the world, where they can produce their products most cheaply and sell most easily.

In the 1960s and 1970s, there was a strong UK regional policy that attempted to steer development to the parts of the country that needed it most. These included much of Scotland, the north of England and Wales. The policy had three objectives: to encourage what used to be called 'mobile industry' in the UK to choose locations where there was unemployment and a need for new growth; to encourage new businesses in such locations to start and to grow; and to attract overseas investment to these areas. That policy had significant success but, because it did not eliminate the regional problem, it was not given the credit it deserved. The policy was largely abandoned in the 1980s, especially the objective of steering growth to locations within the UK that were disadvantaged, and it is not now realistic to think of going back to it. But the attraction of inward investment continues, as does the encouragement of new business growth.

Policies to Assist Growth

Scotland has the institutional infrastructure to tackle this. Grants and loans are available from a variety of sources. In particular, Scottish Enterprise and Highlands and Islands Enterprise are both able to help new firms and existing businesses to grow and South of Scotland Enterprise, which became operational in April 2020, has been added to assist growth in the Borders and Dumfries and Galloway. The Scottish Investment Bank (SIB), an arm of Scottish Enterprise, working also with the other two enterprise agencies, has helped companies to secure funding for investment.

To these bodies has now been added the new Scottish National Investment Bank (SNIB). It came into operation in November 2020. It will absorb the work of the existing Scottish Investment Bank but has a wider role. MSPs have agreed three core aims: driving the move towards net zero emissions, to help mitigate climate change; promoting inclusive growth; and addressing demographic change. It is to invest in employment, housing, education and local regeneration, stimulate innovation to increase productivity, raise skill levels and develop a healthier population. Quite an agenda! The Scottish government is to provide £2 billion to the bank over ten years.

The bank is expected to provide 'patient capital' to help firms that often find it difficult to borrow money over the longer term of 10 to 15 years. It is to support ambitious companies and important infrastructure projects. It is not yet clear what kind of return the bank is expected to earn on its investments. In the early days of the Scottish Development Agency (the predecessor to Scottish Enterprise), there was much emphasis, at Treasury insistence, on the SDA's investments being on a commercial basis. And it was not always easy to see how its funding was to fit in with funds available from commercial banks and other funders, if an element of subsidy was to be avoided. It was argued that there was a gap in the market, particularly for equity, that the SDA could help to fill. But this aspect was heavily criticised by the Conservative government of the 1980s, especially when some of the investments did not turn out well or failed to earn what could be regarded as a commercial return. This role – especially the ability to provide equity – was then curtailed by Ministers. Presumably it is intended that the SNIB will take over this aspect of their work from Scottish Enterprise and the other agencies but it certainly goes against the market fundamentalism or libertarian philosophy of some prominent UK government Ministers. It may, therefore, encounter some of the same criticisms and attract a lot of political attention from opposition parties and others in the UK as well as in Scotland. But, because it will be responsible to Scottish Ministers, it may be less likely to result in its actions being curtailed.

How it will handle its three main roles will only become clear with time. But the COVID pandemic will leave a lot of perfectly viable businesses heavily indebted and in danger of becoming insolvent. This may result in 'zombie' businesses unable to expand or invest for lack of funds. The SNIB could perform a very useful role here by helping such companies to survive either by arranging debt/equity swaps or simply providing long-term loans at low interest. This would be important and of great benefit to the Scottish economy. It is somewhat ironic that the plans for the SNIB, which go back some years, should turn out to be particularly appropriate because of this sudden major illness.

Specific Corporate Headaches

(1) Burntisland Fabrications

The Scottish government already has some problematic investments. The government took a one-third shareholding in Burntisland Fabrication (BiFab), an engineering company with bases at Methil and Burntisland in Fife and Arnish Point on the Isle of Lewis, when it announced that it was going into administration. A rescue was mounted by JV Driver, a Canadian company, and, to assist this, the government provided £52 million in support, in addition to taking a shareholding. But the company went in to administration again. BiFab is one of Scotland's main facilities making structures for the offshore wind industry but it has found it difficult to get work against what it asserted were government-owned businesses abroad and subsidised competition, both inside and outside the EU but notably from the Far East. There may also be an issue of scale and a need for investment in that some of the competitors abroad benefit from a much larger volume of work. BiFab had a £2-million contract to supply turbine blades for the Neart na Gaoithe wind farm project in the outer Firth of Forth but this contract collapsed, apparently as a result of a lack of assurances on future funding.

The loss of this company would be a really serious matter because, without it, much of the work in supplying structures for Scotland's offshore wind industry will come from abroad. At one time, it had been claimed, not unreasonably but especially by SNP politicians, that Scotland's offshore wind industry could be a major source of engineering work in Scotland, just as offshore oil had been. This ambition is now in tatters and the Scottish government must accept much of the blame for a serious failure. When it took its one-third shareholding, there were many assurances about future prospects but what was lacking was a proper strategy agreed with the Canadian owners for the future – how to make it competitive for the long term; how to develop the business; and how to win work from the major offshore developments in prospect. If competition from abroad is subsidised, as is asserted, that should be contested and would justify a measure of protection for the Scottish industry. It should have been raised with the EU if competition from a company in a member state was subsidised.

One cannot imagine the French government allowing one of its companies faced with such obvious and important opportunities to go out of business. Attempts have been made to blame JV Driver for lack of commitment but they say they were not prepared to hand over more money without assurances from the Scottish government. This will not do. There should have been agreement from the start about funding for the longer term. During the development of North Sea oil, the Offshore Supplies Office in Glasgow was set up to ensure that a substantial amount of the work came to the UK. While some opportunities were missed, it was, in general, very successful in achieving that and something similar is perhaps now required.

Offshore wind is of course not the same in that the oil companies, who were always keen to be considered for future oilfield licences, were made aware of the need to place contracts in the UK in the belief that this might help in their bid for licences. The UK government is of course now much less inclined to try to influence companies' decisions than was the case in the 1970s and the Scottish government has had to work with the UK when dealing with contracts for offshore wind. But offshore developments still require planning approval, which should give government a point of entry into decisions. The two governments have said that they could not provide further financial support under EU rules. But this is very unsatisfactory. The ability to supply Scotland's offshore wind industry is one of the most obvious opportunities for the Scottish economy and the government needs urgently to consider how it can achieve this. As matters stood, not only were the facilities and associated employment likely to be lost but the Scottish government would also lose a substantial amount of public money.

In February 2021, as I was writing this, however, it was announced that InfraStrata, a company based in London, was to acquire the Methil yard in Fife and the Arnish yard on the Isle of Lewis of BiFab but not the Burntisland yard. They say they now plan to create up to 1,000 jobs across the two yards, 600 of them in Fife and 400 in Lewis with additional apprentices. InfraStrata also has facilities in Belfast and at Appledore in Devon and the Scottish yards will trade under the Harland and Wolff name. InfraStrata is to pay up to £850,000 for the BiFab assets in two tranches, the second payment to be made depending on the turnover achieved. Obviously this is very welcome news and it must be hoped that a success can now be made of the business. The Scottish government's earlier intervention can, therefore, be credited with saving the yards from closure but it is likely to lose heavily on its one-third shareholding in the previous company and the £52 million it had provided in support.

(2) Prestwick Airport

The Scottish government also has an important investment in Prestwick Airport, having bought it in 2013 for £1 to prevent it closing with substantial loss of employment. The airport has a particularly good weather record and, in the past, this enabled it to be open when other airports were closed because of fog. It has a long runway, which made it suitable as the main airport in Scotland for long-distance international flights. But that has changed since the development in the 1960s of Abbotsinch as Glasgow's airport replaced the former Renfrew airport and, in the 1970s, the building of a new runway and expansion of Turnhouse Airport near Edinburgh. The pea soup fogs that used to be an issue at Glasgow are now also a thing of the past. These things have all resulted in loss of business for Prestwick and it has been struggling to attract custom for more than 20 years. There needs to be a proper analysis of the possible future for Prestwick and whether it is now needed, especially as modern planes, with the ability to land in all sorts of weather conditions, and the concern over climate change suggest reduced opportunities.

The Scottish government has invested over £40 million to

keep it going but there must be a question over the wisdom of this. The airport is seriously underused and is, therefore, a continuing source of anxiety. It had been hoped to sell it to the owners of Glasgow and Aberdeen airports but that fell through. The Scottish Minister for Transport, Michael Matheson, says he still hopes to sell it and there were, at least before the pandemic, some interested buyers. In early 2021, there was, apparently, a preferred bidder but the present position is unclear and there is thought to be a problem, perhaps over repayment of the funds that the Scottish government lent to keep the airport in business. The future therefore remains uncertain. While its loss would be serious for Ayrshire, it should not be continually supported with public funds only for political reasons.

(3) The Ferry Contract with Ferguson Marine

Ferguson Marine at Port Glasgow, Scotland's only remaining merchant shipyard, is another source of anxiety. It is a yard with a long history and has successfully built many ferries for Caledonian MacBrayne (CalMac) in the past, as well as other vessels. But it fell into administration and was rescued when it was taken over by Clyde Blowers Capital in 2014, a company that had been built up by Jim McColl, who is on the panel of advisers to the Scottish government. The company had previously taken over and successfully restored viability to several other engineering businesses in the Clyde valley. Fergusons then won a £97 million contract to build two sophisticated ferries for the state-owned Caledonian Maritime Assets Ltd (CMAL). These vessels were to be dual fired – oil and liquefied natural gas (LNG) – and were intended for the CalMac routes from Ardrossan to Brodick in Arran and from Skye to Tarbert and Lochmaddy in the Outer Hebrides. This contract, however, has turned into a poisoned chalice. The ferries are four years late and will cost at least twice the original price. Perhaps the vessels were too complicated and the dual firing may have caused special issues.

Ferguson Marine say that CMAL kept making alterations to the design and refused to discuss significant increases in cost caused by these changes. CMAL say there was failure with suppliers. Whatever the cause, it is a sorry tale. The Scottish government had provided loans on a commercial basis of £45 million but, in 2019, nationalised the yard after the directors filed for administration for a second time. A new manager, Tim Hair, was put in to sort things out and paid an astonishing £2,565 a day, one of the highest paid public servants in the UK. Most of Ferguson Marine's previous management then left with a loss of their knowledge and expertise. They say there could have been a good future for the yard and, apart from the ferries, there were several opportunities open for other work that have now been lost.

It is not clear what will now happen. Will the ferries actually be completed and, if so, what will be the eventual cost? Was it wise to nationalise the yard? Jim McColl didn't seem to think so. He has said the company did not need saving and that it had a talented management team. He blamed Scottish Ministers for failing to invest in the yard. Did the fault lie with CMAL, also state owned, for making design changes and refusing to agree the consequent costs? The result was that the government assumed responsibility but to what purpose? Might it have been possible to agree a way forward with McColl, with his company retaining the responsibility, even if more financial help was required from government? As it is, even if the ferries are eventually completed, it looks as if the cost to the Scottish government will be very high. But apart from the cost, it would be a tragedy if this apparently troublesome contract were to bring an end to merchant shipbuilding in Scotland.

(4) Liberty Steel and the Fort William Smelter

In the spring of 2021, the future of Sanjeev Gupta's company Gupta Family Group (GFG) Alliance was at risk because it had lost the support of its financial backer, Greensill Capital, which had become insolvent. GFG Alliance's subsidiary, Liberty Steel, had acquired substantial assets in the UK steel industry, including the Dalzell and Clydebridge plate rolling mills in Scotland and another subsidiary of the group, Alvance, had acquired the aluminium smelter at Fort William. The steel plate rolling mills at Dalzell, Motherwell, and at Clydebridge, Cambuslang, are all that is left of Scotland's once large steel industry and, if they were lost, that would be a serious blow, leaving Scotland with no steel industry.

The Fort William smelter is all that is left of the aluminium industry after the closure of the large smelter at Invergordon in 1981 and the Kinlochleven smelter in 2000, all of which had originally been owned by British Aluminium. The industry uses a very large amount of electricity in the process of producing aluminium. When the company had started in Scotland with a smelter at Foyers on Loch Ness at the end of the 19th century, it was, therefore, powered by its own hydroelectricity. It then built the Kinlochleven smelter in 1909 and the one at Fort William in 1929, both also using their own hydroelectricity. The Invergordon smelter had been linked to the Hunterston B nuclear power station, from which it used about a third of the output.

The Fort William smelter, although small compared with smelters in other countries, was a good business with one of the best hydroelectric power schemes in Scotland. Sanjeev Gupta's GFG Alliance, through its subsidiary Alvance, had acquired the smelter and its linked hydroelectricity plant for a reported £330 million in 2016 and the Scottish government had provided a 25-year guarantee, for which the cost in public funds over the period could be substantial, to underwrite the price of hydroelectricity. GFG Alliance had used substantial loans from Greensill Capital to finance its takeover of the steel and aluminium plants. But Credit Suisse has now forced Greensill into insolvency, as it tries to recoup its loans to the company and has begun court action that could force Gupta's business GFG Alliance into insolvency too because GFG owed Greensill £3.6 billion before the latter collapsed.

At the time of writing, it was far from clear how this is likely to end. GFG had asked the UK government for a £170-million bailout but this was refused, apparently due to lack of transparency at GFG Alliance. Meanwhile Sanjeev Gupta has said on television that all his businesses are sound and there is no danger to them. But clearly this is a worrying situation that threatens the existence of an important part of the remaining UK steel industry and what is left of the steel and aluminium industries in Scotland. Obviously the UK government has the main responsibility for dealing with it but the Scottish government's guarantee in support of the Fort William aluminium business could prove very costly. It would be tragic if these plants were to close with loss of jobs and consequential unemployment. It is, therefore, essential that the two governments do their utmost and cooperate in trying to find a solution.

Conclusion

Apart from the problems with GFG Alliance and its ownership of the steel and aluminium plants, where the UK government has the main responsibility, these cases do not reflect well on the Scottish government's ability to deal with industrial issues. There seems to have been a lack of proper planning, unwillingness to face up to difficult decisions and, above all, no Minister or officials with the ability to negotiate tough but imaginative solutions with the companies and deal with them properly. If Scotland becomes independent, it will certainly be necessary for policy on industrial problems to be developed and substantially improved. When a business is in difficulty, it is not enough and may not be wise just to take it into public ownership. Action is required to solve what has caused the problem in the first place. Consideration should perhaps be given to establishing a special body within government to hold investments made by government in companies, rather as the UK government did when it took equity shares in the banks after the 2008–09 financial crisis. This is perhaps a role intended for the new Scottish National Investment Bank but, if so, it needs to acquire the ability and expertise to handle such cases not just as a financial holding company but also with the ability to sort out difficult industrial problems.

In the meantime, to assist the economy, it is absolutely essential, as discussed in an earlier chapter, that education and training produce people with the appropriate qualifications and skills to take advantage of any opportunities that are available. In the same chapter, I also emphasised the importance of improving the provision of vocational training.

At the time of writing, the Christmas agreement on a free trading arrangement for the future relationship with the EU has only recently been agreed and it is too soon to say how it will work out. This, on top of the chaos caused by the COVID pandemic, makes the future economic prospect especially challenging. This may well increase further the chances of a disillusioned Scottish electorate voting for independence in a referendum. But, if so, a worse moment in which to go for something that will cause further upset is hard to imagine and that may make people cautious before risking something else that will cause difficulty and uncertainty.

Independence would have a major effect on the economy. Separation from the rest of the UK would result in major problems and adjustments, which have been discussed earlier. If an independent Scotland can regain membership of the EU single market that would improve investment prospects in time, though by how much and how soon it is impossible to judge. In my book, *Scottish Independence: Weighing up the Economics*, I also drew attention to two other features of the Scottish economy where I would like to see change.

When compared to some other parts of the UK, there has been relatively poor growth from small companies and new business start-ups in Scotland, despite a lot of hard work and effort that has been put into this by the enterprise agencies. Indeed, it was partly for this reason that Scottish Enterprise and its predecessor, the Scottish Development Agency, were set up. Part of this role will now presumably fall to the Scottish National Investment Bank. But both on training and on helping small and medium-sized firms, there appears to be something to be learnt from Germany, the country with the strongest manufacturing sector in Europe. In Germany, there is a well-recognised system of training and also a close relationship between companies and the financial sector – what is known as the *Mittelstand* – which is an outstandingly important feature of the economy. Its success could well repay study by those in Scotland responsible for trying to improve the growth of the economy.

Industrial takeovers in Germany are a much less frequent feature of the economy. In the UK, by contrast, to guard against takeover bids, managements have an incentive to distribute the highest possible dividends, thereby pushing up their share price and making a takeover less attractive to a potential bidder. While it is certainly true that takeovers in certain circumstances can be beneficial – for example, in enabling small firms to get access to capital for investment or expertise needed to allow them to expand and take advantage of opportunities that they might otherwise lose – this is not always so. Many UK companies have been taken over by foreign companies with no noticeable benefit to the British economy – the takeover of Cadbury by Kraft Foods (now known as Mondelez International) being an example. The takeover of Scottish Power by the Spanish company Iberdrola, while not damaging to consumers or employees in Scotland, does not appear to have provided significant benefit either. But more seriously the takeover of Scottish and Newcastle Breweries by Carlsberg and Heineken has resulted only in the loss of a major Scottish company. Some companies, such as Baxters of Fochabers and Walkers of Aberlour, only avoid being the subject of what could be damaging takeovers because they are privately owned. The sad story of the Scottish banks is part of the same problem. Bank of Scotland was a good and well-run bank but apparently fear that it might be subjected to a bid was a factor in its decision to seek a merger with Halifax.[3] Although a merger, it then came under Halifax control. Its subsequent problems were due more to unwise management decisions after the merger than to the merger itself. Royal Bank of Scotland, on the other hand, started its expansion by taking over other companies until its disastrous takeover of ABM Amro brought about its own collapse.

These mergers and takeovers resulted from pressure to reward shareholders or sometimes, one suspects, from managers who want to enlarge their own importance and salaries. The pressure to reward shareholders rather than consumers or employees is an aspect of the short-termism that is a feature of the modern UK economy and can be at the expense of investment in future growth. My conclusion is that such mergers and takeovers are too easy and that some justification should be required, showing benefit to consumers, employees and to the economy, before they are allowed.

6

North Sea oil and gas –
a lost opportunity

One of the biggest differences in Scotland's financial position since the 2014 referendum has been in the expected value of revenue from the North Sea. At that time, it could be credibly suggested that revenue from oil and gas might be sufficient to cover any deficit there might be in Scotland's budget and also to make up for any deficiency in the current account of the balance of payments. Whether or not that was the case then, it is not true now. What happened to the oil revenues is examined later in this chapter but undoubtedly the UK government's treatment of North Sea oil revenues was a huge wasted opportunity.

In 1974, when I was Chief Economic Adviser at the Scottish Office, I wrote a briefing paper for Scottish Ministers which was obtained a few years ago and made public by someone from the SNP under freedom of information. This paper seems to have become notorious and has sparked much comment and controversy. I had forgotten about it until it was unearthed. But because of the attention it has received and the importance of what has happened since, I will set out in this chapter the circumstances. It was written as a confidential briefing for Ministers after the first 1974 election was called but before a new government took office. It is standard practice for officials to use this time during an election campaign to prepare briefings for the new Ministers of whatever government will be elected.

I argued that the then outgoing Conservative government in their public statements had underestimated the financial importance of the developments in the North Sea and, in particular, I forecast that the tax revenues could, by 1980, be very large – much larger than any estimate previously given. The oil companies were doing an amazing job in extracting the oil from deeper water than ever and from an extremely hostile environment in the North Sea and the outgoing government had laid stress on the need to extract the oil as quickly as possible, because of long-standing problems with the balance of payments. But, although they had considered what they needed to do to get as much revenue as possible, I doubt if they had realised how large the revenue could be and no decision had been taken by the time of the election on how this should be done. The choice was between part national ownership – 'carried interest' – as the Norwegians had done with Statoil, a state-owned company that took a part share in their oilfields to secure a share of the revenue; or a special tax to secure an adequate revenue for the state. Their failure to take a decision was partly no doubt because of the Conservative Party's ideological objection to state ownership and reluctance to put up taxes. But they had been heavily criticised by the Public Accounts Committee for failing to take action before the fourth round of licences had been allocated to companies. The Department of Trade and Industry had estimated the output of oil expected in 1980 at 100 million tonnes, which turned out to be reasonably accurate, although it continued to rise substantially thereafter and did not reach a peak until 1999.

Up to that point, all that outgoing Ministers had said was that government revenues from rent and royalties from oil and gas were expected to be about £100 million by 1980. Nothing was said about corporation tax and, under the rules then applying, companies could offset any tax liability from the North Sea with expenditure elsewhere. The SNP had argued that oil revenues for the state in 1980 should be of the order of £800 million, which had been dismissed as a wild figure, but I said in my paper that all that was wrong with it was that it was much too low and that, if the appropriate measures were put in place, revenues could be of the order of £1,500 million to £3,000 million.

There have been suggestions in the press that my paper was suppressed or in some way hushed up. This was not so. It was a confidential briefing for Ministers and never intended for publication, just as other briefing papers for Ministers are confidential. Anyway, the Conservative government lost office in the election. If criticism is warranted, it is not over its failure to provide forecasts for the public but the failure to take the necessary steps to secure an appropriate share of the revenue for the state.

The incoming Labour government quickly took steps to remedy the situation. It set up the British National Oil Corporation to take part ownership in the oilfields and introduced petroleum revenue tax. So far as I recall, it did not publicise the revenues it expected from these measures but that may have been because they depended not only on the expected output but also on the oil price, both of which were extremely uncertain. The oil revenues were quite modest throughout the 1970s, as development continued, but the oil price continued to rise and the volume of oil produced became substantial. Once these measures had been put in place, therefore, revenues rose to an actual figure of £3,700 million in 1980–81 – even more than I had forecast in my paper – and then rose further in the early 1980s, reaching a peak of £12,035 million – over £25 billion in today's prices – in 1984–85.[1] Thereafter, the oil price fell quite sharply, reducing the revenues substantially, although output continued to rise and, during the 1990s, they were averaging about £2,500 million a year. They reached another peak of over £12,000 million in 2000–09 and were £6,145 million in the year before the 2014 referendum.

The Scottish government had estimated oil revenues in their White Paper for the 2014 referendum at between £8 billion and £9.2 billion in the years 2014–15 to 2017–18, whereas the Office for Budget Responsibility (OBR) had much lower estimates of £4.6 billion to £3.9 billion for the same years.[2] The Scottish government's estimate was based on an oil price of $113 per barrel for Brent crude but they had a second set of estimates based on a rising price that was considered quite likely. There was also an expectation that output of oil would increase, following major investment in the North Sea and particularly to the west of Shetland. As events turned out, however, all these estimates of oil revenues were far too high.

The oil revenues for Scotland since 2014 are as set out in Table 4. As will be seen, this was very different from what was forecast in 2014, even using the more cautious OBR forecast of that time. So what happened? The international price of oil was halved and, far from being $113 a barrel, averaged $51.8 in the five years 2015–20. In 2015–16, repayments of petroleum revenue tax actually exceeded the revenue, resulting in a negative figure. The outbreak of COVID in 2020 then caused the price to be extremely volatile, sometimes very low and then recovering. It rose to over $60 a barrel in February 2021, though that was still well below what had been expected in 2014.

**Table 4: Scottish Geographical Share of
Government Revenues from North Sea Oil Production**

Year	£ million
2014–15	2,254
2015–16	-318
2016–17	159
2017–18	1,142
2018–19	1,358
2019–20	844
2020–21	550

Source: 'Government Expenditure and Revenue Scotland 2020–21',
Scottish Government, Edinburgh, August 2021.

The oil price will undoubtedly fluctuate in future, as it has in the past, but it seems unlikely that the revenues will ever reach the high levels seen previously. Even if oil production continues to be significant for a considerable number of years, as is expected, it is well past its peak and expected to continue a gradual decline. Furthermore, it will get increasingly expensive to produce, as exploration moves into deeper water and less productive fields are developed. Climate change and policies to combat it will also have an effect, as there must be an increasing move away from fossil fuels towards reliance on renewables. While revenues from oil will still be valuable and may rise again for a while, they can no longer be counted on to cover a deficit in the Scottish government's budget. Pressure to review existing licences in the light of concern for climate change can only reinforce this conclusion.

So, if the boom in North Sea oil is past, what is there now to show for it? The UK resources of oil and gas were as significant as those of Norway but, unlike Norway, no fund was set up into which the revenues could be held for the future. The Norwegian sovereign wealth fund – or, to give it its proper name, Government Pension Fund Global – was founded in 1990 and, in December 2020, it was valued at £923 billion or £170,000 per person in Norway. It is invested 72.8 per cent in international equities and 24.7 per cent in both fixed interest government bonds and bonds of international companies. Ironically, it rose by £90 billion in 2020 because the stimulus from central banks pushed up asset values at a time when other countries, such as the UK, were having to greatly expand their debt.

In the 1970s there was talk of setting up a UK fund and there was a good case for it. The issue was considered by Cabinet and Bruce Millan, then Secretary of State for Scotland, and Tony Benn, then Secretary of State for Energy, both argued for it. But the country's economy was in a very bad state at the time. Inflation was extremely high, peaking at 25 per cent in 1975. Government finances were in an alarming state as a result of a tripling of the international oil price and were made worse by the miners' strike in the coal industry, both of which caused inflation. The government had been forced to seek help from the International Monetary Fund. The Treasury's view was that it needed the revenue from North Sea oil and could not afford to put it aside into a special fund. All this was, of course, in the 1970s before the substantial UK oil revenues had started and was understandable at the time. In 1979, the government changed and the incoming Conservative administration regarded the defeat of inflation as its main priority. This it achieved by adopting a very tight monetary policy which, in addition to the coincidence of major oil revenues starting in 1980, forced up the value of the pound on international markets. This made companies unable to compete against their foreign rivals with the result that unemployment rose, reaching a peak of 11.9 per cent of the labour force in 1984 with 3 million out of work. This would have been catastrophic for the public finances but was, in effect, paid for by the large revenues from North Sea oil. So the oil revenues ended up paying for the unemployment.

And now, if the oil bonanza is over, what do we have to show for it? The Scottish economy is undoubtedly much stronger than it was in 1974. Employment in oil-related activities, mainly but not exclusively centred on Aberdeen, made the north-east of Scotland one of the wealthiest parts of the UK. There were benefits for industry and employment in other parts of Scotland too. This offers part, but only part, of the explanation why Scotland has done significantly better than Wales or many of the English regions over these years and why it now has a GDP per head that is exceeded only by London, the South-east and the East of England. Investment to develop North Sea oil resulted in major improvements in infrastructure to assist development, mainly in the 1970s: the upgrading of the A9 to Inverness and the A90 to Aberdeen; the major development of the airports at Aberdeen, Inverness and Sumburgh; the reinstatement of dual tracks on the railway to the north between Blair Atholl and Dalwhinnie and the retention of the railway from Inverness to Kyle of Lochalsh, which was to have been closed but was kept open in the expectation it might be needed for the building of oil production platforms requiring the deep water of Loch Kishorn; and a big investment in housing around Aberdeen, the Moray and Cromarty Firths and in Shetland.

Had an oil fund been set up in the 1980s, which would have been the time to do it, because that was when the revenues were particularly high, who knows what might have been achieved? It would, of course, at that time have been a UK fund, rather than a purely Scottish fund, but it could have been given instructions to give special attention to Scotland. I have heard Nigel Lawson, the former Chancellor, say that there was no point in setting up a special oil fund because the oil revenues enabled the national debt to be reduced. But, in fact, the national debt was 37.8 per cent of GDP in 1980, the Conservative government's first year of office, and

36.6 per cent in 1997 when they left, so not a huge difference. But, in any case, this is to miss the point. The oil revenues were used to finance ordinary public expenditure, whereas the argument for putting them in a special fund was so that they could be used to fund either the modernisation of the economy or kept for some other special purpose.

In my 1974 paper, I had argued that Scottish industry needed investment to modernise and be able to compete with its counterparts in Europe, having just joined what was then the European Common Market. Investment had been held back by repeated stop–go policies as a result of problems with the UK balance of foreign payments. I argued that this would no longer be the case. I also argued for strengthened regional policy. But none of this fitted the philosophy of the government of the time. There was no mention of an oil fund in the 1980s.

What has happened instead was what I recall Denis Healey calling 'a holocaust of manufacturing industry' and then a continuing decline. Was this necessary? Much of the decline in the older industries was inevitable and happened in all the advanced countries as their economies moved to services but, in my opinion, it was too brutal and some at least of the businesses, including those from overseas that had come to Scotland, could have stayed if conditions had been more favourable. Many, of course, will say that what happened in the early 1980s was necessary, that the power of the trades unions, which had so damaged the economy in the 1970s, had to be curbed and that many of the businesses that closed had to go anyway, because they were inefficient and no longer able to compete on world markets.

But, had an oil fund been set up, it could have been used to strengthen the economy and, if much of the proceeds had been invested internationally, as the Norwegians did with their fund, it would have helped to prevent the pound from rising to the point at which so much of manufacturing was uncompetitive with rivals in other countries.

Some of what might have been done is illustrated by the Shetland and Orkney oil funds. The Shetland fund — the Shetland Charitable Trust, formerly the Shetland Islands Council Charitable Trust — was the result of some very hard bargaining by the then Chief Executive of Shetland Islands Council, Ian Clark, and this resulted in a 'disturbance payment' being made in respect of the volume of oil that flowed through Shetland's Sullom Voe oil terminal. A similar scheme was then also applied to the smaller terminal on the Orkney island of Flotta. The benefits of this are plain to see — the Shetland trust has paid £320 million to island charitable activities since it started. As well as greatly improved infrastructure in Shetland, there are superb leisure and sports facilities for young people throughout the islands, excellent care homes for the elderly and the purchase of fishing quota for Shetland fishermen.

But, if the setting up of an oil fund was an opportunity missed, it is now long gone. If Scotland becomes independent, there is no use harking back to what might have been. Oil may still play a significant but smaller part in Scotland for many years yet but, with the resource dwindling and concern for climate change now an increasingly important issue, Scotland has to look to other resources, of which it is fortunate to have many, to generate its energy. These also offer major opportunities and policy must now be directed at ensuring that these are used for the benefit of Scotland and her people.

The prospects for energy supplies

The future for energy in Scotland now looks very different from how it appeared at the time of the 2014 referendum. Apart from North Sea oil and gas where, as Chapter 6 has shown, the prospects are much poorer than was then expected with greatly reduced revenues and lower levels of output, there have also been major changes elsewhere in the sector. The possibilities for the future, however, have been thoroughly examined by a Royal Society of Edinburgh Inquiry, chaired by Sir Muir Russell with a powerful committee of leading experts in the field.[1] The resulting report provides a major source of information on the prospects and possibilities for the future.

The situation is, of course, complicated by the division of responsibility between the Scottish and UK governments. Formally, the UK government has the responsibility for energy policy under the 1998 Scotland Act but the Scottish government has responsibility for planning decisions and could refuse permission for new developments such as a new nuclear power station. Wind farms, though initially for local government to decide, rest ultimately with Scottish Ministers to approve if they are over 50 megawatts (MW). This, therefore, requires the two governments to work closely together and can give scope for one to blame the other in case of difficulty. But, if Scotland becomes independent, all such decisions, together with the financial implications that its decisions would involve, would, of course, be entirely for the Scottish government.

In 2015, some 51 per cent of energy in Scotland was required for heat, 25 per cent for transport and 24 per cent for electricity generation.[2] These figures are not likely to be very different now. But the emphasis is much more strongly on reducing carbon output to combat climate change. Partly in response to this, there is an ever-increasing emphasis on energy-saving measures. Total energy consumption in Scotland fell by over 13 per cent between 2007 and 2019. There has been the start of a move away from conventional forms of energy in transport, where we have seen the introduction of hybrid powered buses and cars and increasingly fully electric vehicles; on the railway, there is also more electrification. But this process still has a long way to go. Several car manufacturers have announced their intention to switch manufacturing to entirely electric vehicles in the relatively near future. Advances in battery technology, combined with the much greater availability of charging points, are making this possible. District heating schemes and ground-source heat pumps can be expected to play an increasing role in heat for buildings, especially larger buildings where they can promise considerable savings. There is also likely to be a move to electricity in place of gas or oil for heating, though cost is a factor here. Efforts are constantly being made to improve insulation in buildings, although there is still much to be done and retrofitting old buildings, such as houses, is expensive and often far from easy.

Many of the changes that are likely point to a need for a substantially increased output of electricity. But switching to electricity, of course, only helps in combating the CO_2 emissions that are responsible for climate change, if fossil fuels are not required in the electricity generation. Here major progress has been made and Scotland's electricity generation has undergone immense change since the 2014 referendum. In 2019, just over 61 per cent of electricity generated in Scotland was from renewable sources. This was equivalent to close on 90 per cent of all electricity used in Scotland but excluding net exports to England and Ireland. On the other hand, only 6.5 per cent of non-electrical heat was from renewables and very little energy in transport was green, so the increase in electricity from renewable sources, while impressive, only amounted to 24 per cent of total energy consumption.[3]

Within the electricity industry, there have been immense changes. Scotland's two large coal-fired power stations, Longannet and Cockenzie, have both closed. At the time of the 2014 referendum, there was no suggestion that Longannet would close. It was the largest power station in Scotland and had been adapted to burn gas to replace 20 per cent of the coal. It was also able to burn environmental waste such as sewage sludge. There had been a proposal for carbon capture at Longannet to be linked to storage in the North Sea in some of the oil fields but this was rejected by the UK government on grounds of cost. There had also been suggestions that Scottish Power might rebuild Cockenzie as a gas-fired station. Together the two power stations had a capacity of 3,600 MW and they were able to meet a large part of the demand for electricity in Scotland. With both of them gone, the supply of electricity now has to come from elsewhere.

There are now no deep coal mines operating in what was once a major Scottish industry and none of Scotland's electricity is now derived from coal-fired generators. The two nuclear stations, Hunterston B and Torness, are nearing the end of their lives. Hunterston B is due to close in 2023 and Torness in 2030. When they were both operating with a combined capacity of 2,600 MW, they produced about a third of Scotland's electricity supply. The hole in Scotland's generating capacity that has been caused by the closure of the coal-fired power stations will, therefore, become even larger when the nuclear stations close. But, so far, there are no plans for any replacement nuclear capacity and, indeed, the Scottish government is opposed to further investment in nuclear power, despite the fact that its generation – although, admittedly, not its construction – is carbon free.

The only fossil-fired power station now left in Scotland is at Peterhead, a plant originally designed to burn oil but converted to gas to take advantage of the nearby terminal at St Fergus, where very substantial amounts of gas were brought ashore from the North Sea. Originally, Peterhead burned waste gas from the Brent oilfield, before the construction of the Mossmorran plant in Fife enabled it to be processed. This power station has undergone many changes. Originally intended as a 1,320-MW plant, its conversion to gas and a major repowering project resulted in its capacity being increased to 2,407 MW – much the same as at Longannet – although it was later reduced again to 2,177 MW. Nevertheless, with this capacity, it remains a major part of the electricity system in Scotland and, unlike the two large nuclear stations, there is no date for its closure. It could, therefore, end up as the only large power station in Scotland after 2030.

To replace the coal-fired power stations that have closed, there has been a huge increase in electricity generation from renewables. Hydropower has, of course, been an important part of Scotland's electricity system since the 1950s, when the majority of the present dams and power stations were built and, with an overall maximum capacity of over 1,400 MW, it remains an essential contributor. The Glendoe Hydro Scheme of 100 MW near Fort Augustus, which was opened in 2009 by the Queen, is the most recent addition to the capacity. There is some scope for further developments, especially to meet peak-load demand, although many of the best resources are now used and environmental opposition to new schemes is likely to be much greater than in the 1940s and 1950s. Recently, a number of small 'run of river' schemes have been constructed by private operators with encouragement from the government and these should continue to be supported.

The biggest increase in renewables capacity, however, is in the generation of electricity from wind. Electricity generated from wind has become progressively cheaper as it has developed and onshore generators are now the cheapest source of new capacity. It does, however, suffer from two major drawbacks.

Firstly, they require a lot of space and this creates a considerable environmental impact, especially visually. Opposition to such developments is strong in many areas and there is no doubt that they do change the scenery of Scotland and, in some cases, they also raise concern from the Royal Society for the Protection of Birds (RSPB). It is important that local communities that are affected benefit financially from such developments. There has been less opposition to offshore schemes although there can be environmental problems with them too – especially because of the effects on birds and the higher costs entailed.

The second problem is that the load factor for onshore wind is often less than 30 per cent overall, though some of the newer ones achieve a lot more. Offshore wind is better but still normally less than 50 per cent.[4] This varies with location. The availability of wind in Shetland, for example, gives a higher load factor than on the mainland. It also varies with the age of the equipment, with older turbines tending to gradually lose their efficiency. This means that wind power, despite improvements constantly being made to the efficiency of the turbines, cannot be relied on to meet requirements every day. It, therefore, has to be backed up by another source of power, even if in total there is the ability to generate more electricity than is needed. Electricity demand also varies greatly, depending on temperatures and time of day, with peaks in winter especially on cold mornings. This has always meant that the capacity has to be able to meet the peak demand, even if much of it has to stand idle for a significant amount of time.

The importance of hydroelectric power and pumped storage

The hydro stations are extremely valuable in dealing with

this. Many of them are designed with a high capacity to meet peak rather than base load, which enables them to be turned on at very short notice, so that peak demand can be met. However, they have insufficient storage capacity in their reservoirs to allow them to be in operation all the time. The two pumped storage schemes at Cruachan and Foyers, with a capacity of 720 MW, are designed specifically for this purpose. When electricity demand is low, they are able to use off-peak electricity to pump water up to their reservoirs from Loch Awe and Loch Ness respectively. This means that they have sufficient water in their upper dams to generate power at full capacity in peak hours. The Coire Glas scheme, proposed by SSE, near Loch Lochy and approved in the autumn of 2020 by the Scottish government, though still awaiting commercial approval, was revised from an original 600 MW scheme and enlarged to 1,500 MW maximum. When built, it would double Scotland's pump storage capacity.[5] It would then be the largest scheme of its kind in the UK. Since electricity cannot readily be stored, these schemes enable the water resource used to generate it to be stored instead. This works well for daily variations of peak and off-peak demand but is obviously less able to cope if the variation is of much longer duration because of lack of wind. The Coire Glas scheme, however, according to reports, will be able to generate for 24 hours without a break, once completed.

There are other schemes that have been proposed. The Hamilton-based Intelligent Land Investment (ILI) Group have secured planning approval for a new pumped storage scheme at Dores on Loch Ness and the Drax Group, who bought the existing Cruachan scheme in 2018, have announced proposals to greatly increase its capacity with a new power station underground. All of this is encouraging but such schemes are extremely expensive and require a lot of capital. It remains to be seen whether they will be judged viable and then go ahead.

Pumped-storage hydro schemes are helpful and important

but other ways of storing electricity will be needed, if the bulk of primary generation is expected to come from wind. This also applies to any electricity that might be generated from the sun, using photovoltaic panels as, given the Scottish climate, this would also be variable. Tidal stream energy, which is being pioneered in Orkney and the Pentland Firth, is less irregular but is still at the very early stage of development. There have been considerable advances in battery technology in recent years and an example is that Fair Isle in Shetland now has a 24-hour electricity supply from wind turbines backed up with battery capacity, which has replaced two diesel generators.[6] Battery development is promising as a means of storing electricity and there are likely to be further improvements in the technology and reductions in cost.

The potential of hydrogen

The Scottish government, however, has also given considerable attention to the development of hydrogen technology as a means of dealing with the variability in electricity supply from wind.[7] A lot of work is being done and the technology is quite well established.[8] What is known as 'blue hydrogen' can be derived from natural gas, using a process known as steam methane reformation but this process has to be backed up with carbon capture and the pumping of the CO_2 to a safe reservoir if it is to be acceptable as a means of providing clean energy. BP was proposing to do this at Peterhead, using the offshore reservoir of the Miller field for storing and disposing of the CO_2, but eventually the company gave up in frustration while waiting for UK government approval. This was unfortunate to say the least. But it is a possibility for the future and could be used to supply hydrogen for domestic purposes instead of the current natural gas – methane. The other method for producing hydrogen is by using an electrolyser to separate oxygen and water to leave the hydrogen. This is known as 'green hydrogen' but it requires a lot of electricity.

This was the type of hydrogen produced in the Shetland island of Unst several years ago and the entrepreneur responsible then used the hydrogen to power his car. Hydrogen, once produced, can be used to give power from fuel cells to make electricity or used directly as a fuel. It can also be stored if required and transported.

There are plans from the North of Scotland Hydrogen Programme, a consortium that includes the Port of Cromarty Firth, Scottish Power, several major whisky producers – Diageo, Glenmorangie and Whyte & MacKay – and Pale Blue Dot Energy, who are leading the project, for a hydrogen hub on the Cromarty Firth. The project would use wind power from several nearby offshore fields with an electrolyser in the Firth to produce hydrogen.[9] The hydrogen would be used in several of the distilleries but is also seen as something that could point the way to meeting Scotland's ambitions for its climate change targets and providing a supply of green energy for the future. Already there are buses running on hydrogen fuel in Aberdeen. There are also some local hydrogen hubs throughout Scotland, including at Methil in Fife, Aberdeen, St Fergus in Aberdeenshire and Orkney and plans for some of the islands. It is expected that the technology would become cheaper as it develops scale and could be used eventually to export energy from Scotland. With new electric cables being approved to link Orkney and Shetland, as well as the Western Isles, to the Scottish mainland, it would be possible to use wind power on the islands to link with hydrogen hubs. This could also enable the wind power from these sources, where availability is often greater than on the mainland, to produce hydrogen. It could then be transported to wherever it was needed. These proposals to develop the use of hydrogen are exciting as they could make Scotland a major source of green energy based on its wind power, enabling hydrogen to be used whenever required and exported if necessary.

All this is still at a very early stage and, as is often the case with ambitious projects, unforeseen problems may well arise.

But it could develop quickly. Five years ago, it was scarcely thought of and, in another five years, it could either have come to nothing or be a major project for Scotland. The issue is whether this is sufficiently promising to avert a lack of regular and reliable power when the nuclear power stations close. Although Hunterston B is scheduled to close in 2023, Torness, which is a much newer station, is expected to remain in production till 2030 and may be extended further. That could give time for the developments expected in battery technology and hydrogen to progress to the point where the need for a new major power station is avoided. But that cannot be counted on as certain and the Scottish government needs to have a plan B if, ultimately, these proposals end in disappointment. Indeed, given that the nuclear stations may close quite soon, it is surely a major criticism of the present government that such a plan has not already been developed and made publicly available. Scotland, at present, exports electricity both to England and to Ireland and only needs to import it when one of the present nuclear stations has to be closed for maintenance and there is insufficient supply from renewable sources. But that could change after both nuclear stations close and it would be undesirable to have to rely on a regular imported supply, especially as England itself may have to import from Continental Europe.

If a new major power station is eventually necessary, how could this need be met without wrecking the Scottish government's ambitions for clean energy and keeping to its targets for climate change? The options would appear to be either a new gas-fired generating station, coupled with carbon capture linked to an offshore reservoir for the carbon, or a new nuclear station.

A gas-fired station linked to an offshore reservoir to store the carbon would be similar to what was proposed by BP at Peterhead and which may eventually be acted upon. But it would need to be in addition to the output of Peterhead. Indeed, although there is an issue of cost, which has concerned the UK government, it seems unfortunate that the proposals for carbon capture linked to reservoirs in the North Sea first at Longannet and more recently at Peterhead have not so far been acted on. It is only by building such a plant that the technology can be tested and the cost eventually be reduced. A new large nuclear station would take up to ten years to build. The experience over Hinkley Point C in England, which is to be a large 3,200 MW station owned by the French national company EDF Energy, is not reassuring either on the time that it would take or the cost. The latter has been estimated at £23 billion and may turn out higher.

There is a possibility, outlined in the RSE report, that small modular nuclear reactors with generating capacity of 300 MW may have a part to play in future. It is suggested that, because of their scale, construction could be more efficient, less expensive and more easily financed. Their viability and performance are being investigated by the UK government and the Nuclear Decommissioning Authority. Four reactors of this type are apparently in an advanced stage of construction in Russia, China and Argentina. It is thought that they could utilise existing UK plutonium stocks as fuel, which would be a considerable benefit and help to reduce the proliferation of waste. But, like so much else in the energy field, it will be many years before it is clear whether they could offer a sensible solution for Scotland. Meanwhile, nuclear waste remains an unresolved issue. The intention is that it would eventually be buried in deep underground caverns but, so far, it is only temporarily stored as no really satisfactory solution has yet been found. This is a powerful reason against building a large nuclear power station, at least until this issue is solved to an extent that satisfies public opinion.

The hope must be that the need to go down this route can be avoided and that the Scottish government's ambition to provide adequate energy from renewable sources can be realised. But in view of so much uncertainty, it is not enough just to hope that all will be well. Both the Scottish and UK governments have a responsibility and really must work together. They need to explain to the public how they intend to ensure that Scotland has a secure energy supply for the future and to set out the steps they would have to adopt to secure it. It is regrettable that, as yet, that has not been done.

The financial sector

Scotland's financial sector is a very important part of the economy. It employs some 85,000 people directly and, according to estimates, the same amount indirectly. It contributes about 8 per cent of GDP. If Scotland were to become independent, what happens to it is, therefore, of great importance. There could be some beneficial effects if Scotland, through being either in the EU or the EEA, was to be again in the EU single market. But there could also be adverse effects if Scottish financial institutions have to overcome a barrier when trading with the rest of the UK. What the net effect would be is not easy to forecast at this stage.

The Banks and their Problems

Many people have commented that an independent Scotland could not have coped with the financial crisis in 2008–09, when the two major banks, Bank of Scotland and Royal Bank of Scotland, were in danger of insolvency. That is undoubtedly true. They were both in danger of going out of business and had to seek help from the UK government. The Irish government had to seek help from the IMF and the EU when its banks got into trouble and a condition of the assistance was the imposition of extreme austerity, much more extreme than anything imposed on Scotland by George Osborne,

Chancellor of the Exchequer in the coalition government of 2010–15.

That, of course, assumes that the government of an independent Scotland had done nothing to impose stricter regulation on the banks. The problems were a consequence of the UK government's 'big bang' in the 1980s, which deregulated the financial sector and enabled UK commercial banks to engage in activities such as investment banking, that previously had been reserved for specialist investment or merchant banks. It also unleashed a spate of takeovers and mergers. But very few people saw the crisis coming. Indeed, Alex Salmond, Scotland's First Minister at the time, was enthusiastic about the Royal Bank's continual expansion, a bank he had previously worked for.

The crisis at the two big banks was a serious blow for Scotland, whose banking sector had had a reputation for sound financial management and a distinguished history. The Bank of Scotland was the oldest bank in Britain apart from the Bank of England, which is one year older. It was founded in 1695, several years before the Act of Union. The Royal Bank was founded in the 18th century, allegedly because of suspicions of Jacobite sympathy in Bank of Scotland. Both banks had absorbed several other Scottish lenders, notably the British Linen Bank in the case of Bank of Scotland and the Commercial and National Banks of Scotland in the case of the Royal Bank. They had survived relatively unscathed when there were major bank failures in England in the first half of the 19th century. They retained the right to issue their own bank notes, thanks largely to a campaign headed by Sir Walter Scott, when the English banks lost that right as a result of repeated bank failures.

But both banks had significant proportions of their shares owned by English banks. In Bank of Scotland's case, this dated from the takeover of British Linen Bank, which had been wholly owned by Barclays, and, in Royal Bank's case, from takeover of the National Bank, which had been owned by Lloyds. Royal Bank, in particular, had been subject to Lloyds trying to increase its shareholding with a view to mounting a takeover. The big bang of the 1980s increased this pressure as takeovers became a more likely danger, despite the fact that the Monopolies and Mergers Commission (MMC) had signalled it would not approve takeover of the Scottish banks on competition grounds and because of adverse effects in Scotland.

In the early 1980s, however, Standard Chartered Bank, based in London but with substantial international business made a bid for Royal Bank, which the Royal Bank board signalled it would accept. Before this could happen, the Hongkong and Shanghai Banking Corporation (HSBC) made a rival and significantly higher bid, which the Royal Bank board decided to resist. This became a major issue in Scotland. Both bids were then referred to the MMC. The Scottish Development Agency argued against the bids in evidence to the MMC and I, as head of the Industry Department in the Scottish Office, gave evidence to the MMC on behalf of the Secretary of State for Scotland. I argued that the financial sector was of major importance to the Scottish economy and that, if the Royal Bank lost its independence, we could expect a bid to be made for Bank of Scotland in the near future too. We thought there was a serious risk that it would weaken the Scottish financial sector if the banks lost their independence and became subsidiaries of banks outside Scotland. Much of their ancillary activities could then be conducted outside Scotland. There was conflicting evidence from the Governor of the Bank of England, who did not feel that he could adequately influence HSBC, which was a major world bank, and the Foreign and Commonwealth Office, which argued that it would be wrong to discriminate against HSBC and in favour of Standard Chartered because HSBC, though based in Hong Kong, was a British Bank. In the end, the MMC accepted the argument of the Scottish Office and concluded against both takeover bids.

All of this is ironic in view of subsequent events. The Royal Bank's management was greatly strengthened and, in late 1980s, it took over an American bank and the much larger English bank, NatWest. These takeovers appeared to be successful but Royal Bank then seriously overreached itself with a bid, together with the Fortis Bank based in the Benelux countries, for the Dutch bank ABM AMRO, at a time when there was already a recession looming and with insufficient checking of the financial state of ABM AMRO. With the American financial scene suffering from the subprime mortgage affair, the result was disastrous. Royal Bank came very near to insolvency and had to be rescued by government taking an 82 per cent shareholding and with a major cash injection of £42 billion. Royal Bank remains part-owned by the state. The present management have changed the name of the group back to NatWest Group and, although technically its headquarters are still in Edinburgh and it will continue to trade as Royal Bank of Scotland in Scotland, it is now effectively a UK bank with its main base in London.

In the meantime, Bank of Scotland decided it should try to increase its size so that by expanding its deposit base, it could increase its lending. It also seems to have been motivated by fear that, unless it became larger, it would be the subject of a takeover by a larger bank. It had also tried unsuccessfully to bid for NatWest and, when that failed, it tried for a merger with the former building society Abbey National. It proved impossible to agree terms and Bank of Scotland eventually agreed a merger with the much larger Halifax. Halifax had been the largest UK building society but, along with most of the other building societies, had demutualised and converted to a bank. Although it was a merger rather than a takeover and the headquarters was in Edinburgh, Halifax, as the bigger partner, was dominant and supplied the Chief Executive. Despite its huge loan book as a former building society, the management pressed for further expansion and when the financial crisis came, Halifax Bank of Scotland (HBOS) was threatened with insolvency. The government then encouraged a takeover by Lloyds Bank. But this got Lloyds into difficulty so that the government again had to assist by taking a shareholding in the merged company. This has now been repaid but the consequence is that Bank of Scotland is now a subsidiary company in Lloyds Banking Group.

To those who, like me, were proud of Scotland's banking history, this is a sad story. But it simplifies the position if Scotland were to become independent. Scotland's two largest banks would be subsidiaries of large UK business groups. Both would be based in London and, although the registered offices are in Scotland, that would soon be changed. Even if one of these large banking groups got into trouble, which is now unlikely, that would not be a problem mainly for Scotland. In the event of such a scenario, the Scottish subsidiary could be split off and that might require action from the Scottish government, but there would be no responsibility for what happened elsewhere. This is in contrast to the situation when both large banking groups were effectively Scottish banks. The rule is that if, like the Icelandic bank Landsbanki, it operated branches in other countries, the parent bank is then responsible for compensating depositors of those branches in those countries in the event of difficulty. But if, like the other Icelandic bank Kaupthing, it operates in that country through a subsidiary company regulated in that country, the parent bank has no such responsibility.

The responsibility for compensating depositors elsewhere in the rest of the UK would, therefore, not arise with the two Scottish banks as subsidiaries of major UK banking groups. The same would apply to Clydesdale Bank which is, at present, in the process of becoming part of the group headed by Virgin Money. There are also the UK's challenger banks, including Tesco Bank and Sainsbury's Bank, that have set up in Scotland in recent years. There is, however, a lesson to be learnt for the future from the big two, Royal Bank and Bank of Scotland. If an independent Scotland ever again has a Scotland-based bank that is doing business in the rest of the UK or in other countries, it needs to do it through a subsidiary company that is subject to a regulator in those countries.

Asset Management and Life Insurance

Important though the banks obviously are, it is in asset management that Scotland has specialised and built up its special reputation for finance. According to the UK government's analysis in 2013, whereas Scotland had 8.7 per cent of the UK's employment in banking and 8.1 per cent in insurance, it had 11 per cent of the UK's employment in fund management.[1] In 2017, this industry had £615 billion under management. Some 7,500 are employed directly in the industry and a further 5,500 are supported by the industry. A large number of firms are involved, among which are Standard Life Aberdeen, Baillie Gifford, Kames Capital and Blackrock. There are also many UK and international firms with asset-servicing activities that have offices in Edinburgh. Related to all this are risk managers, accountants and people involved in back-office roles. In view of its importance as a major centre for asset management, it is obviously important that this is retained in Scotland.

It is not yet clear what effect Brexit will have on the sector. Financial services were not included in the free-trade deal – the EU–UK Trade and Cooperation Agreement (TCA) – negotiated by the UK government at the end of 2020 and there are already signs of some parts of the activity moving from London to other financial centres, such as Amsterdam, Dublin and Luxembourg. An important issue is how EU 'passporting' will be affected. Passporting enabled British companies to trade across the whole of the EU single market, as if it were the home market, and also enabled foreign firms from outside the EU to trade in the EU single market by establishing a base in the UK. Essentially, it meant that, if a firm met the regulatory requirements of the authorities in one EU country, it could trade across borders with other EU member states. According to a paper by Jeremy Peat and Owen Kelly, 5,500 financial services companies passported their services out of the UK into the EU and 8,000 passported their services from the EU into the UK in 2016.[2]

A paper written by Sarah Hall for UK in a Changing Europe at the end of 2020, immediately after the TCA was concluded, pointed out that the agreement did very little to facilitate access to the EU single market for financial services. From 1 January 2021, UK firms would, therefore, lose their passporting rights.[3] Around 40 per cent of the sector's exports go to the EU, so this could have a major effect. In order to continue with their exports, firms would have to either meet the different requirements of individual EU states or rely on equivalence decisions from the EU. Trying to meet the separate requirements of individual states would be complex and time-consuming at the very least and equivalence does not cover core-banking services, such as lending, nor does it guarantee permanent access, because the EU can withdraw equivalence rights with 30 days' notice. It does, however, offer the prospect that equivalence decisions could be made relatively quickly, especially as the EU Commission has indicated that it could be one of the areas where decisions may be made within what are described as a set of 'pillars of cooperation' with the EU. The upshot of all this is that, at the time of writing, there is still a lot of uncertainty on how Brexit is going to work out for the UK financial sector.

If Scotland became independent and was able to join either the EEA or the EU, the single market for financial services would be restored. The EU might be concerned that Scotland could be used as some sort of backdoor entry for UK firms to trade in the EU single market. There would have to be safeguards to prevent this but a consequence could be that, rather than UK financial businesses opening offices for their activity in Dublin, Frankfurt or Amsterdam, they might do so in Scotland instead. In view of the importance of the sector and its ability to generate significant tax revenue, the Scottish government would be expected to encourage this. But how big this effect might be can only be a subject for speculation at present. On the other hand, there would also be a danger, especially if Scotland adopted its own currency, as I have argued in Chapter 3, that some of the businesses presently in Scotland might decide to move to a base elsewhere in the UK. This would probably be especially likely for those businesses that had the bulk of their customers in England, such as life insurance companies where policies are often linked to mortgages. Their customers might be unwilling, indeed unwise, to face exchange rate risk. This is also why there is very little cross-border pensions activity between the UK and other countries at present. Fund managers might be less likely to be affected than life insurance companies but many people would probably feel happier if their stockbroker was based in the country where they live and this could affect those who deal directly with a fund manager rather than through a broker. This could especially apply if there were tax complications involved in the cross-border transfer of funds.

So the conclusion must be that, at this stage, it is impossible to predict how this would work out and, in particular, whether the benefits of Scotland being in the EU single market for financial services would outweigh whatever negative effects there would be from loss of business as a result of separating from the rest of the UK. Unlike manufacturing, tariffs would not be an issue but differing regulations could be a major one. Furthermore, it needs to be recognised that the Scottish financial sector, as it presently operates, is largely an offshoot of the City of London and that would gradually change if Scotland chose to become independent.

Institutional Changes

A number of new institutions would also be required if Scotland was to become independent. If the pound sterling was retained at least for a while, there would probably need to be a currency board, just as Ireland had for some years after its independence, but this could lead to the creation of a central bank. A central bank would certainly be needed if Scotland set up its own currency, which, as I have argued, would probably be necessary and could, in the end, be advantageous (see Chapter 3). This would require expertise and skilled staff to manage monetary policy, including interest rates and the issue and management of debt. The central bank would also have a role in managing the exchange rate between the Scots currency, the pound sterling, the euro and other currencies.

Once the currency had found a level that ensured the economy was competitive, it should then be pegged either to the pound or the euro to avoid unpredictable fluctuations. The Danish krone is pegged to within a 2.25 per cent band with the euro. Once a peg is fixed, it would be for the Scottish central bank to manage the Scottish currency to ensure that the peg was maintained. That would require the avoidance of excessive deficits on the balance of foreign payments but currency reserves would be needed to deal with inevitable fluctuations. That is why it would be important in the negotiations with the rest of the UK that Scotland was able to get a share of the UK's currency reserves along with other assets (see Chapter 3).

In addition, to ensure that banks and other financial businesses avoided risk and were properly managed, there would need to be a financial regulator. After experiencing what happened to the Icelandic and Irish banks during the 2008–09 financial crisis and the need to avoid anything similar ever happening in Scotland, this would be a priority. Apart from the Bank of Ireland, the other Irish banks are all still nationalised as a result of that crisis. The setting-up of a financial regulator could result in the employment of lawyers and accountants in the private sector.

There would need to be a money market and facility for foreign exchange trading. Because of Brexit, Scotland might have aspirations to rival Ireland as a financial sector refuge from London. But it would need to be borne in mind that Dublin already fills that role and it would be difficult to find something special that could differentiate Scotland advantageously. Ireland being in the euro area would be less subject to currency movements. Even if the Scottish currency was pegged to either the pound or the euro, there would always be a risk that unexpected forces might force the peg to be changed (see Chapter 10 for the dangers of being in the eurozone). Ireland has the further advantage for many businesses in that it is a low tax country, whereas many in Scotland seem, for understandable reasons, to favour the Scandinavian higher tax and higher spending type of economy. It would be very difficult to compete with Ireland on tax, even if that was the aim of a Scottish government. Ireland's corporation tax rate is only 12.5 per cent and, for multinationals shifting global profits to Ireland, it is even lower. But this has incurred a lot of opposition from other EU countries and, although Irish governments have managed to maintain it, it is hard to see the EU accepting such a rate in another country, whether a member state of the EU or a member of the EEA.

There would need to be a Scottish stock exchange, which could attract business from companies north of the Border. But most of the capital that needed to be raised would probably continue to be done in London or internationally, either in continental Europe or New York.

These institutional changes and innovations could result in the creation of a lot of jobs, many of them important and highly paid. But they would also involve substantial cost from public funds. This, coming at a time when Scotland was trying to balance its budget after a period of deficit while it was in the UK, could require difficult decisions to be made.

Conclusion

The widely expressed fear that an independent Scotland would not be able to handle a major crisis affecting its banks, like the one that occurred in 2008–09, should not now be a worry as the major lenders are all subsidiary companies of major banking groups based in London. The Scottish banks, as subsidiary companies registered in Scotland, would be subject to a Scottish regulator and they would be responsible for the deposit guarantee for their depositors in Scotland but not for those elsewhere so the concern that might have existed in 2014 would no longer apply.

The asset management industry is a particular strength in Scotland and, if Scotland was a member of the EEA or the EU, it would be in the EU single market with passporting rights across the whole EU. This would be an advantage, although how much of an advantage compared with the rest of the UK depends on what arrangements are eventually agreed for the UK financial sector trading in the EU. Against this, there would be some firms presently based in Scotland that felt that, because the bulk of their customers were in other parts of the UK, they should move there. Only with time will it be possible to see how substantial these effects are.

There would be significant employment and some large incomes for those in key jobs in the new central bank, the financial regulator and the stock exchange.

Mortgages and pensions[*]

There has been understandable concern about the costs and security of pensions and mortgages if Scotland were to become an independent state. Would pensions continue to be paid as they are now? Would interest rates on mortgages be higher or lower or remain the same as for the remainder of the United Kingdom? There are serious issues here that it is the aim of this chapter to explore. They do not arise if Scotland remains within the United Kingdom, even if more devolution or federalism is introduced, but, if there is a prospect of independence, it is quite understandable that they worry people.

Mortgages and Borrowing in an Independent Scotland

The Council for Mortgage Lenders have said that having to comply with separate legal and regulatory systems would increase costs and could, therefore, lead to more expensive mortgages in Scotland. Owen Kelly, former chief executive of Scottish Financial Enterprise, citing similar reasons, said to me some time ago that the cost of mortgages would be

[*] In this chapter, I am updating and amending some of the text of Chapter 9 in my book *Scottish Independence: Weighing Up the Economics* (Birlinn, Edinburgh, 2014).

likely to rise.[1] In one of the economic analysis papers of the UK government in 2014, the Treasury pointed out that mortgage lenders would be likely to face increased costs in raising funds on the wholesale market. If so, that too would increase the cost of mortgages in Scotland. All of this suggests that the cost of mortgages and, indeed, other borrowing would be higher in an independent Scotland. As the Treasury paper pointed out, a one per cent increase in the mortgage rate for a 75 per cent mortgage on the average house price in Scotland could add some £1,500 to the annual cost.

Much would depend on whether there is still a fully integrated financial sector and common interest rates across the UK border. Even if Scotland shares the pound on a sterlingisation basis with the rest of the UK, that does not remove doubt. The rest of the UK would be most unlikely to agree to have common sterling debt with Scotland for government bonds because that would mean that taxpayers in Scotland and the rest of the UK would stand as guarantors for each other's debt. That would give Scottish borrowing a free ride on the financial credibility of the rest of the UK. Since the eurozone was established, that is what has so far proved unacceptable to member countries and prevented the issue of common eurozone bonds. Each country is, therefore, still responsible for its own debt and it has resulted in the market losing confidence in the debt of weaker members. Huge interest rate differentials then opened up when the financial crisis developed.

If there is no common sterling debt, as seems likely, Scotland's government would have to issue its own bonds. Theoretically, the interest rate on Scottish bonds could be either higher or lower than on UK bonds. In practice, however, Scottish bonds would be most unlikely to have lower interest rates than UK bonds because they would be a new issue on the market for which there was no previous record. If Scottish government bonds had a higher interest rate, as seems likely, however, that would be reflected in wholesale market costs for mortgage lenders.

If sharing the pound on a sterlingisation basis was abandoned or decided against, Scotland would need to introduce its own currency. But that would also give rise to the likelihood of differences in interest rates. Even if the Scots pound was pegged to sterling, this would depend on how the markets judged the respective security of the Scottish and UK currencies.

With separate currencies, even if they are pegged, there is always the possibility that market pressures or differences in economic performance may force exchange rates to be altered. That introduces exchange risk and is the reason it is very unusual for mortgages or personal loans to be cross-border. To owe money to a lender in another country with a different currency can be dangerous. If, for example, the Scottish currency were to depreciate, it could become more expensive to pay back a loan in sterling, if that was the currency in which it was borrowed. Of course, if the Scottish currency appreciated in value, the borrower would gain but, with the boom in oil revenues that could push up the value of the currency now over, that seems unlikely. In the past, there were examples of some companies operating in Scotland with loans from foreign banks – for example, in Deutschmarks – that have been made insolvent as a result. It is, therefore, a risk that no individual should take.

The consequence would be that mortgage lenders operating in Scotland would establish branches or subsidiaries operating in the Scottish currency and new loans would be taken out in Scots pounds but those already holding loans would still have them in sterling, while the assets to which they related – a house or a flat – would have a value in Scots pounds. This would be risky if, at any time, the exchange rate between the two currencies were to change. Those holding loans or mortgages in sterling would, therefore, be well advised and might be required by mortgage companies to have them converted into Scots pounds. There might also be a significant number of people with mortgages or personal and small business loans from English lenders that did not have a presence in Scotland. In such cases, the borrowers would be subject to exchange risk and they should then be advised to pay off their loans and take out fresh ones with companies operating in the Scottish currency.

As a consequence of the COVID crisis and the earlier financial crisis, the Bank of England's lending rate to the other banks was at its lowest since the Bank was founded in 1694. It is bound to rise eventually to more normal levels and that will have an impact on the rates for mortgages, whether provided by banks or building societies. Scotland would be affected in the same way as the rest of the UK but, with its own currency, lending rates would be more likely to differ. Freedom of capital movements would mean that the Scottish central bank would be bound to have regard to rates in the rest of the UK in setting its own rates, just as the Bank of England at present takes account of rates set by the European Central Bank and the US Federal Reserve. There would be a strong possibility that there would be a premium on Scottish rates over and above the rates elsewhere, as tends to be the case for other small countries.

So there is a considerable number of uncertainties for mortgage holders and other borrowers in Scotland, if Scotland becomes independent. Unless there continued to be full integration in financial services with common interest rates across the border, which seems most unlikely, especially if there is a new Scots currency, it is hard to avoid the conclusion that there would be some increase in the cost of borrowing. And, if there was a separate currency, maybe not at the start but in due course, exchange risk would necessitate a reduction in cross-border borrowing. Mortgages, personal loans and loans for business would then have to be taken out in Scottish currency, which would probably be possible only from lenders, whether banks or other mortgage companies, operating in Scotland.

How Secure Would Pensions Be?

Much more has been written about pensions in an independent Scotland than about mortgages. The Institute of

Chartered Accountants in Scotland (ICAS) raised questions about the future of Scotland's pensions in April 2013.[2] The Scottish government, at that time, published a substantial paper in which it sought to allay these concerns in the event of independence.[3] But, since the publication of that paper, the issues and anxieties have been further elaborated by the National Association of Pension Funds (NAPF).[4]

Pensions are not an easy subject for the average citizen to get to grips with. Indeed, for young people, as I remember well from my early days as a university lecturer in Glasgow, it all seems complex and unreal. Eyes tend to glaze over as experts try to explain it. The frequent changes that have been introduced do not make it any easier. But pensions are important and those who do not pay the subject enough attention early in their careers live to regret that when they come to retire.

The subject divides into three parts. First, there is the existing state pension. Would it continue to be paid in an independent Scotland as at present? Second, how would the many public sector employees in the civil service, the National Health Service and in teaching, hitherto paid directly or indirectly by the UK government, receive their pensions? And, finally, private and company pensions depend on funds built up by the companies and financial institutions and these have to be paid out when the insured person reaches the agreed retirement age. It is over this last group that the most concern has been raised.

The State Pension

The state pension, although notionally contributory through National Insurance, is paid out from general taxation. But it is important to recognise how easily changes with serious consequences can be introduced by governments, whether the UK government or a potential Scottish government. Because it is unfunded but paid out of current tax revenue, the pressure on public finances has to be balanced against obligations to pensioners and others who receive public funds. The many changes that have been made over the years illustrate this very clearly.

For example, in the 1980s, payment of the old-age state pension, which had previously been increased annually in line with average earnings, was altered to be up-rated annually using the Consumer Price Index instead, as a cost-saving measure by the then Conservative government. This saved a substantial amount of public expenditure at the expense of pensioners. In response to the concern that this caused, the Labour government introduced a further change in 2002. The pension would be increased annually either by 2.5 per cent or by the inflation rate, as measured by the Retail Price Index, according to whichever was the higher.[5] This was supplemented by the means-tested Pension Credit for people whose income on the pension alone was inadequate. Then, in 2010, the Coalition government changed the system again, introducing what is called the triple lock, which was to apply until at least 2015.[6] However, this is still the situation at the time of writing. It increases the state pension annually by whichever is the greatest – the increase in average earnings, inflation as measured by the Consumer Price Index or 2.5 per cent a year. But there could be further changes by the UK government, as it seeks to restore public finances after the COVID crisis, especially as inflation has generally been below the 2.5 per cent by which pensions have been increased in recent years.

Despite these changes, the state pension is still one of the lowest state pensions in Europe.[7] In contrast to many other European countries, the tradition in the UK has been to rely heavily on the private sector, either as company occupational schemes or private pensions that individuals have invested in with life assurance companies. According to the Scottish government's 2013 independence white paper, however, only about half the Scottish population was covered by occupational or private pensions and the situation is unlikely to have changed much since then. To the remainder, without any occupational or private pension, the state pension, though not generous, is crucially important.[8]

The UK government, as well as introducing the triple lock for up-rating the state pension, introduced a new single tier state pension in April 2017. This replaced the previous complex system, which included the Second State Pension, contracting out, Pension Credit and various out-of-date additions. Up-rating of this new system will be decided from year to year but the triple lock system continues at present. In 2020–21, the full state pension is £175.20 a week – £9,110.40 a year. This is paid to those who have made national insurance contributions for 35 years. For those who do not have the full 35 years of contributions, there will be a pro rata reduction, subject to a minimum qualifying period of ten years. However, in line with forecasts for improved life expectancy and to make the cost of the pension sustainable, the qualifying age was raised from 65 to 66 years by October 2020 and is to rise further to 67 between 2026 and 2028. In his Autumn Statement of 2013, the then Chancellor said he expected the qualifying pension age to go on rising to 68 in the late 2030s, 69 sometime in the 2040s and with the prospect that it could rise to 70 after 2050. A review of the state pension age is to be carried out every five years to ensure that the costs are shared fairly between the generations. Although life expectancy is expected to continue to rise, the problem is that many older people suffer from chronic health problems that make them unfit or unable to work as they once did.

The Scottish government's proposals, as set out in the 2014 independence white paper, were to build on the UK government's scheme.[9] They were set to be slightly more generous and the triple lock was to continue for the life of the first Parliament after independence. The Scottish government accepted the UK government's increase in the state pension age to 66 in 2020 but proposed that any further increase should be subject to review by an independent commission to take account of Scotland's lower life expectancy.

There was a strong flavour of political manifesto about these proposals. Although the differences were not very great, there was an undisguised attempt at each point to offer something better than the UK government. Like political manifestos generally, however, it would, in the event, depend on what could be afforded. Past experience has shown that governments do not hesitate to make changes, if compelled to do so by economic circumstances and, since 2014, the much lower level of North Sea oil revenues than the then Scottish government was forecasting does not suggest that it will be easy to avoid a fiscal deficit, especially as Scotland's demographic structure imposes additional burdens.

Public Sector Pensions

Like the state pension, most public sector pensions are unfunded – only the Local Government Pension Scheme (LPGS) is operated as a funded scheme. For many of the unfunded schemes, employees and employers pay contributions but there is no dedicated fund into which these are paid and then invested. In total, these contributions may either exceed or fall short of the amounts to be paid out in a particular year. Where this is so, the balance is either paid over to or made up from UK government tax revenues, in the case of the NHS and teachers' schemes; and by the Scottish government in the case of police and firefighters' schemes.

The operation of the NHS and teachers' pension schemes is handled by the Scottish Public Pensions Agency for which financial management responsibility rests with the UK Treasury. The Local Government Pension Scheme is managed by 11 local authorities and the schemes for police and firefighters are also locally managed. But all of these schemes must comply with UK legislation. Only in the case of a small number of public bodies – certain judicial office holders working for devolved bodies and its own members – does the Scottish Parliament have policy and legislative control.

Pensions for the civil service in Scotland and for the armed services are paid by the UK government and are entirely under the control of the UK Parliament.

With independence, responsibility for paying all of these pensions would transfer to Scotland. The Scottish government have given an assurance that those already retired, as well as those who will retire in future, will have their pensions fully protected. Where a person who has worked in the public sector in Scotland – a civil servant, for example – retires to live in England, payment of his or her pension would also be made by the Scottish government. But there are, nevertheless, important matters to be negotiated. There could be many cases where a retired person worked for part of his or her life in Scotland but the rest in other parts of the UK – for example, civil servants who have worked for a UK department, such as Defence or Employment and Social Security – and responsibility for payment in such cases would be more complicated and would, presumably, have to be shared.

A future government of an independent Scotland would be free to set retirement ages for public sector employees as it saw fit and these might increasingly diverge from ages set in the rest of the UK. In line with the recommendations of the Hutton Commission, there is no proposal to change the unfunded public sector pensions to any sort of funded scheme.[10] Since there is no dedicated fund, there is no question of moving to a Defined Contribution (DC) system but steps have already been taken to move away from Defined Benefit (DB) based on final salary; the DB system was to the advantage of those ending their careers in senior positions with high salaries, since it gave them a pension set as a percentage of final salary. This is now replaced by a pension based on Career Average Revalued Earnings (CARE).

The Local Government Pension Scheme, which is a funded scheme, has assets that give a funding level of 82 per cent of liabilities, having fallen slightly in recent years. Income from contributions has been increasingly less than benefits paid out, the difference now being £75 million. Other smaller funded schemes for devolved bodies are similarly supported by dedicated funds.

Unfunded pension liabilities for the public sector in Scotland, however, are extremely large, even without the substantial liabilities that would be transferred to Scotland for the civil service and armed forces schemes in the event of independence. Defining the Scottish government's responsibility for the civil service in Scotland would be relatively straightforward but it is much less clear how the armed services might be divided and, in consequence, how much of the responsibility and what share of cost would have to be taken over. Like other schemes in the rest of the UK, these unfunded schemes currently pay out more in pensions than they receive in contributions and the gap is expected to grow. With independence, it would be for the Scottish government to decide how this should be handled – for example, whether an increasing amount of the cost should be funded by tax revenue or by increased contributions. Scotland might decide to tackle this differently from the rest of the UK but the implications could be substantial.

Private Sector Pensions

Although occupational and private pensions form a very large part of the incomes of retired people in the UK who receive them, their experience has not been a happy one. Only about half of the Scottish population have such pensions, so that this is one of the main causes of income inequality. Furthermore, participation in such schemes has declined rather than increased although, since 2005, all employers are now under a statutory obligation to enrol employees in a pension scheme and this is enforced by the Pensions Regulator. Private sector pension scheme membership in the UK is less than half what it was in 1967. According to work done by HM Treasury in 2014, membership in Scotland is slightly higher than in the rest of the UK but it has still fallen.[11] Part of the reason for this fall may be the sharp reduction in the percentage of employees in manufacturing industry, where many would have been automatically enrolled, but part may also be due to the disappointing performance – and, indeed, failure – of some of the schemes, which has discouraged people from joining them.

One might have expected private and company pension schemes that are funded to be less dependent on action by government but this is not the case. In the recent past, governments of both major UK parties have intervened in ways that damaged the value of pensions. The Conservative government's Financial Services Act of 1986 ended the requirement for employees to be in occupational schemes. The Act also removed tax exemption on pension fund surpluses. Companies with funds in surplus over what was needed to match their liabilities had been able to deduct the full amount as a cost before profit was assessed for corporation tax. Ending this tax exemption in good times only discouraged companies from building up such surpluses and meant that funds failed to match liabilities when the market suffered a fall. Then, in 1997, the Labour government ended Advance Corporation Tax Relief for pension funds. This change, for which Gordon Brown, the Chancellor of the Exchequer at the time, has been blamed, cost pension funds an estimated £5 billion a year, reducing dividend income by about 20 per cent.[12] Most of the schemes remained profitable, however, until the stock market crashed in 2001. At that point, when the market for equity shares was at its most depressed, the regulator required pension companies to rebalance their portfolios, apparently to safeguard the interest of pensioners. But selling large amounts of equity stock, when the market was already at its lowest for many years, only depressed equity prices further and buying fixed interest stock with these depleted funds pushed up the price of gilts and other bonds. The resulting large loss in value was never recouped.

It is, therefore, not surprising that many occupational and private pension funds were in difficulty from the late 1990s and into the present century. The bankruptcy of the Equitable Life Assurance company graphically illustrated the problem. In the early 1960s, when I was a young lecturer starting my career at the University of Glasgow, I had to choose into which life assurance company I should invest my pension under the then university scheme. The information I was given showed that Equitable Life gave the best return. At its peak it had 1.5 million policyholders and £26 billion under management. But, in 2000, it closed to new business because it had failed to make sufficient allowance for adverse market changes. Attempts to find a buyer failed and a great many policyholders lost a lot of their money. Mercifully, later in my career, I had transferred what I had invested into another pension scheme but many people did not or were unable to do so and were left with pension income amounting to only a fraction of what they had expected.

In 2008, the Parliamentary and Health Service Ombudsman found the government guilty of ten counts of maladministration and called for a compensation scheme. It was estimated that 30,000 policyholders had died without compensation. Many pension companies had assets which were insufficient to fund their liabilities. In time, it was expected that such companies would be able to resolve this by building up their assets and repairing their balance sheets. But, in view of the number of pensioners who had suffered losses, a compensation scheme was put in place.

The Pensions Act of 2004 established the Pension Protection Fund (PPF) in response to public concern when employers sponsoring Defined Benefit (DB) pension schemes – schemes that gave the pensioner a fixed percentage of final salary on retirement – found that such schemes had become insolvent. The Fund provides compensation to scheme members affected by insolvencies and is financed by a levy on participating schemes. Only DB schemes and the defined benefit part of hybrid schemes based in the UK are eligible. Assessment is triggered by the insolvency of a scheme and a valuation is then conducted of its assets and liabilities to see whether the scheme could afford to purchase annuities at or above the level of compensation. Only if it cannot, does the PPF provide compensation, in which case it takes over the scheme's assets. The Scottish government have said that it would expect an independent Scotland to play its full part in these arrangements, but that would need to be part of a post-independence negotiation with the UK government. It might be more likely that a future Scottish government would have to set up a Scottish equivalent to PPF.

But a consequence is that many Defined Benefit (DB) schemes have been changed to a pension based on contribution – Defined Contribution (DC). The Financial Services Compensation Scheme provides compensation to those with Defined Contribution pensions, if necessary, so long as their provider was approved by the Financial Conduct Authority. The change to DC pensions means that what a pensioner will receive will depend on the market – how much he or she has paid into the scheme, how the funds from his or her accumulated contributions have been invested, what they are worth at the time of retirement and what the rate on annuities happens to be at that time. This introduces a huge element of uncertainty. If a person retires when the market is high, he or she could do as well or even better than with a DB pension but, if retirement coincides with a slump in the market, the annuity that could be bought with the maturing fund could result in a disappointing pension, especially if annuity rates are as low as they have been in recent years. Before the financial crisis, almost all companies offering occupational pensions did so on a DB basis whereas, now, almost all offer their employees only a DC pension.

Pension investment as a form of saving has always been encouraged with substantial tax relief. The cost of both occupational and private pensions can be paid from pre-tax income, resulting in a substantial saving of both standard and higher rates of tax. Recently, as a result of the very large earnings some people have been receiving, a ceiling of £50,000 has been imposed on the amount that can be invested in a pension in any one year. Anything above this is subject to tax.

In view of what has happened, it is not surprising that confidence in the industry has been badly shaken and that, over the UK as a whole, a very large number of people are estimated to be under-saving for their retirement. Both private pensions and occupational pensions have been affected. A further problem has been that annuity rates have been very low for several years and there is no sign of them rising in the near future, with the result that money from a pension fund, when invested in an annuity, has resulted in a disappointing pension. This is partly an unavoidable consequence of the Bank of England's unprecedentedly low lending rate to help the recovery of the economy and the Bank's policy of buying gilts as part of its quantitative easing programme. This has pushed up prices and kept interest rates exceptionally low on government stock in which a large part of pension funds is invested. The upshot is that, for many of those who had invested in pensions, the income achievable has been disappointing. In some cases, people who invested have felt misled when their pensions have fallen well below what they had been led to expect by a pension company. There have been accusations of mis-selling and some claims for compensation have been upheld.

The coalition government, as part of its reform of pensions, introduced automatic enrolment in an attempt to address the problem of under-saving. This reverses the provision in the 1986 Act which freed employers from this obligation. Employers now have a duty to enrol all employees, who are at least 22 years old, in a DC workplace pension, unless the employee specifically asks to be exempted, and it is expected that many more employees across Scotland will now be enrolled, some for the first time. However, this process will take time. To help employers fulfil their duty to enrol their employees, the new National Employment Savings Trust (NEST) provides a scheme focused on those with low or moderate earnings. The scheme is also open to those who are self-employed.

The Scottish government said, at the time of the last referendum, that, in the event of a vote for independence, it had no plans for changes to tax relief on occupational or private pensions, it would continue automatic enrolment and it would work with the UK government to ensure that both employers and employees continued to have access to NEST. It also envisaged that a Scottish equivalent to this scheme would, in due course, be set up. Presumably that is still the position.

If Scotland becomes independent, however, there could be implications for pension companies both in Scotland and elsewhere in the UK. If Scotland were to continue to use sterling as the currency on a sterlingisation basis, it might hope that some at least of the UK institutions would continue to operate in Scotland with minimal change. The body of law governing pensions in Scotland would continue to apply until such time as a Scottish government decided to make amendments. This would also apply to the regulatory framework although, after independence, the Scottish government has said it would set up a Scottish Pensions Regulator.[13] It is proposed that this body would work closely with the UK regulator and the UK Financial Conduct Authority.

On the assumption that Scotland would find it was unable to continue to participate in UK institutions, however, separate institutions – or, at least, Scottish branches of institutions based elsewhere in the UK – would then have to be established. A separate currency, even if pegged to sterling, would also introduce considerable uncertainty for pension holders. If the currency peg were at some stage removed or the exchange rate altered, in what currency would pensioners be paid and what might their pensions then be worth? If the pension was taken out with a Scottish pension provider, presumably the pensioner would be paid as before but in the new Scottish currency. If, on the other hand, it was an English scheme, exchange risk becomes involved. The pension, unless arrangements had been made otherwise, would be paid in sterling and that might be worth either less or more in the Scottish currency, depending on the movement of exchange rates. This is why pension schemes generally do not cross national boundaries. Indeed, within the EU, the UK was the home state for only 28 such schemes and half of those were with the Irish Republic.[14]

This problem of cross-border schemes has been highlighted by the Institute of Chartered Accountants for Scotland (ICAS). The EU's directive – Institutions for Occupational Retirement Provision (IORP) – made it possible for institutions to provide pensions across national borders and was intended to be a step towards providing pensions on a European scale. It applies not just to EU states but to the whole EEA. There was a requirement for schemes that are cross border to be fully funded, with assets at least matching their liabilities, but the latest IORP II Directive now has provision for funds that do not meet this requirement to take steps over time towards achieving this. This latest directive also clarifies what is meant by cross border. It applies to schemes that have members in more than one country but not to schemes that only have beneficiaries in a country other than the home country of the scheme. If Scotland becomes a separate state from the rest of the UK but within the EU or EEA, this directive would apply and those schemes with members across borders that are not at present fully funded would have to take steps to meet the requirement. Especially as the rest of the UK would not be in the EEA, they might have to reconstruct themselves into separate Scottish and rest of UK schemes. The danger is, of course, that, if schemes had to comply quickly with the fully funded requirement, a number of them could be forced into insolvency.

Provided there is goodwill and a readiness to compromise, it should be possible to negotiate a transition period for schemes to become fully funded if they do not at present meet this requirement. No one, after all, would think it right for such schemes to be underfunded indefinitely. Nor, presumably, would the rest of the EU think it would be right for this to become a roadblock when the purpose of the directive was not to hinder but to promote the development of an integrated internal market in financial services.

Conclusion

So there are many issues relating to both mortgages and pensions that have to be considered if Scotland becomes independent. For mortgages, without common sterling bonds, rates of interest would be likely to be higher than in the rest of the UK and a separate regulatory system could impose higher costs. A separate currency would also necessitate mortgage borrowing to be reconstructed to avoid the exchange risk that cross-border borrowing would imply. People would then arrange mortgages for their houses or flats either from purely Scottish institutions or with the branches or subsidiaries of the UK institutions that were able to lend in the Scottish currency.

For private and occupational pensions, some of the same issues apply and there is the additional complication of the EU's IORP Directive that requires cross-border schemes to be fully funded although the latest version of the directive, IORP II, provides for a transition period and defines cross border only as where there are members and not just beneficiaries in more than the home state.

The Scottish government gave very clear assurances in 2014 that people with state pensions would not be any worse off in an independent Scotland and presumably this would still be honoured. But no one expects financial resources to be anything other than restricted for years to come, either in

Scotland or the UK, especially after the cost of dealing with COVID. Governments have, in the past, made changes that have left state pensioners worse off and damaged the funds on which private pensioners depend. One hopes that potential Scottish governments would not make changes that could adversely affect pensions. But there can be no guarantee against damaging changes in future, either in Scotland or the UK, because the problem of being able to afford pensions for an ever-increasing proportion of elderly people in the population is one of the pressing issues of our time.

The European Union and its problems

The creation of what has become the European Union had its origins in the determination of leaders, particularly Jean Monnet and Robert Schuman in France, to prevent a repeat of the tragedies of the two world wars. They were the moving spirits in setting up tariff-free trade in coal and steel with the establishment of the European Coal and Steel Community (ECSC) in the 1951 Treaty of Paris. ECSC had six member states – France, West Germany, Italy, Belgium, the Netherlands and Luxembourg. The clear success of integration in coal and steel led, in 1957, to the Treaty of Rome, with the same six countries, which established the Common Market for manufactured products, agriculture and fish. By integrating the economies of member states so that they became interdependent, cooperation would replace rivalry and disputes would be settled by agreed rules. An important feature was that the treaty protected the interests of the smaller countries from pressure from their larger neighbours.

But ending rivalry and the resort to violence between members, which had been frequently the rule over the previous 1,000 years, was not the only aim – important though that undoubtedly was. It was also seen as an important means towards increasing prosperity for all member states. The prosperity of the United States was seen as a consequence, at least in part, of its unity. And now, as a result of the creation of what eventually became the EU, Europe has not only had a longer period of peace than for many centuries, it has also achieved higher levels of prosperity than would otherwise have been possible. This was a signal achievement. Membership was widened in 1973 with Britain, Ireland and Denmark joining. Greece joined in 1981 and Spain and Portugal in 1986. This was seen as helping to secure democracy in the latter three countries, all of which had endured dictatorship before joining. Further enlargements included Austria, Sweden and Finland in 1995 and then, after the end of the cold war, enlargements that included ten countries of Eastern Europe, plus Malta and Cyprus.[1] This enlargement changed the nature of the EU and made its management more difficult but it was strongly supported by the UK. Indeed the UK was among those countries that argued most strongly for the former Communist countries to become members.

On my first visit to the European Commission in Brussels in the early 1960s, I remember being struck by the atmosphere and the determination of those that I met there. 'We are building a new Europe,' they said, 'and it must not be like the Europe of the past. The focus will not be on rivalry but on integration and increasing prosperity.' It was understood that this would be accompanied by a gradual degree of political integration but how far this would go was left to evolve in the future. Indeed, there was a widespread difference of view on what was envisaged. It was suggested by the more enthusiastic that it could end up with some form of federation or confederation leading to a kind of United States of Europe but this was not President de Gaulle's view and it was never endorsed by the UK.

From the start the UK saw the Common Market primarily as an economic arrangement. Perhaps British governments were at fault for not making it clear to the public that there was a political dimension and that it was always intended to become much more than a free trade area. The British attitude, after joining, certainly showed no commitment to this wider vision for Europe and tended to be more about concern over how much the UK contributed financially, as one of the main contributor nations, and how it could get its money back. Because the UK was late in joining the Common Market, the financial system for funding European expenditure had already been put in place and it did not suit the UK well at all. The bulk of the expenditure at that time went on agricultural support and the budget was primarily funded by a mixture of import levies on agricultural products, customs duties and a contribution from VAT. Because the UK had a relatively small agriculture for its size and it was efficient, it stood to get relatively little of the expenditure on agriculture but to contribute a large share of the income, whereas France with twice the land area and a large agriculture was a substantial recipient. This led to a serious problem for the UK but was eventually rectified after Mrs Thatcher took a very strong line at a summit at Fontainebleau in 1984, when it was agreed that the UK would get a substantial rebate. This rebate continued until the UK left the EU, although Tony Blair agreed to some reduction to help finance the enlargement of the EU, when the former Communist countries joined. Arguably the rebate became less justified as agriculture became a less important element in the EU budget, the importance of the structural funds to help growth in disadvantaged areas grew and the funding of the budget was changed. Because the funding was recognised as being regressive, contributions were adjusted to a new system predominantly related to each member state's GDP.

But the UK has also contributed in a major way to making the EU what it has become. The UK – and Mrs Thatcher, in particular – strongly supported the proposals to make the Common Market into a single market with the elimination of non-tariff barriers to trade and she was instrumental in ensuring that a British Commissioner, Lord Cockfield, was given the responsibility of bringing this about through the Single European Act of 1986. This Act also increased the powers of the European Parliament and extended majority voting in the EU Council. The Common Market had eliminated tariff barriers but there were many other impediments to trade between countries, notably regulation over standards, which prevented exporters from getting access to markets in other member states. Indeed, regulations had become more important than tariffs or import duties as a barrier to trade. The aim of the single market was to eliminate these non-tariff barriers not only on goods but also on services such as finance, thereby increasing the scope for international trade between members. Lord Cockfield asked the Italian economist, Paolo Cecchini, to prepare a report on the potential gains from a single market for Europe. His report, 'Europe 1992', showed that the gains could indeed be substantial and, following what became known as the Single Act, these were subsequently obtained.[2]

Implications for Scotland

There are people who say it would be a mistake for an independent Scotland to leave the UK to rejoin the EU, as that would also constrain its scope for action as an independent state. A sizeable proportion of those who support the SNP apparently also claim to be in favour of Brexit. But, in the modern world, all countries are to a degree interdependent, something many of the Brexiteers seem to fail to recognise. The English doctrine of sovereignty – the 'Queen in Parliament', which accords special importance to Parliament and especially the government of the day, usually elected by a minority of the electorate – was based on the work of the Whig jurist A V Dicey. This doctrine is not understood by many other countries, where sovereignty is often divided, as it is in federal countries, nor in Scotland where, traditionally, and traced back to the Declaration of Arbroath in 1320, sovereignty has been regarded as resting with the people rather than the king. In the UK, especially in England, Dicey's view has led to a particular notion of sovereignty and the need to guard it jealously. Membership of the EU, for example, was seen by many as not really compatible with this traditional English view.

But in order to be prosperous and safe, countries have to make agreements with other countries over trade and security and with international bodies such as the UN or NATO. That involves some sharing of sovereignty, and the EU is no different. But there are legitimate questions over the degree of freedom to decide policy that a member state will be prepared to share or accept to be constrained.

While some countries accept the direction of travel towards increasing political integration, many others do not and, as will be seen later in this chapter, if the euro is to be successful, it raises some of these issues. In particular, with the enlargement of the EU, there are many member states that would have serious reservations about moving to a form of federal Europe, in which the identity of individual member states would be submerged. There may indeed be a case for a two-speed EU, in which those that feel able can move further along this path than others. So far, that has been resisted but the issue is likely to come back sooner or later as national identity is not something that can readily be set aside. Indeed, Scotland's experience illustrates this as the feeling of Scottish national identity is still strong more than 300 years since the Act of Union and many would say it is stronger now than it was a hundred years ago. Membership of the EU, while requiring some sharing of sovereignty, certainly does not require as much as the nations of the UK have given to Parliament at Westminster.

The European Union, however, undoubtedly has its problems. Three issues in particular have caused major difficulty which, at times, have led to widespread discontent and even to doubts about the future of the union itself: the enlargement of the membership of the EU; the greatly increased flow of immigrants, especially from the Middle East but also from Africa; and the serious problems that have arisen with the monetary union of the eurozone, notably with Greece but also with Italy, Spain, Portugal and, for a time, with Ireland.

The EU Enlargement

The enlargement, especially to include the former Communist countries, has made managing the EU much more difficult. Indeed, the larger it has become, the more difficult this is. While welcome, the increased number of member states means that it is more difficult to agree on policies. The former Communist countries of central Europe were all keen to join and have received a large amount of financial help. But with the passage of time the initial enthusiasm has worn off and some of them, especially Poland and Hungary, have not only resisted a common policy on handling immigrants but have elected populist governments that have shown autocratic tendencies and threaten the independence of the judiciary in their countries, one of the principles to which member states must subscribe. It is not yet clear how this will be dealt with but it could result in funds being withheld or, in the extreme case, even more drastic measures. It has the makings of a serious crisis.

The Migration Crisis

The problem of large volumes of inward migration has already left the EU in some disarray. Some countries, notably Germany, have accepted a large number of immigrants, conscious of the need to help with one of the most serious humanitarian problems of our times, but also aware that the ageing structure of their own populations would benefit from an inflow of younger people. This, however, has been far from the view everywhere. And undoubtedly concern about Islamic terrorism and simply the difference in cultural background of Muslim immigrants have been factors. This put great strain on the principles of the Schengen Agreement, which provided for passport-free movement between member states and a common visa zone. Schengen was originally a separate treaty but was incorporated into the EU's *acquis communautaire* in the Amsterdam Treaty.

All member states were expected to join the Schengen Area but Romania, Bulgaria and Croatia have not yet done so and the UK and Ireland were given opt-outs. The signatories of the Schengen Agreement are not exactly coterminous with membership of the EU. For example, Norway, Iceland and Liechtenstein are part of Schengen, although not members of the EU, while the Republic of Ireland, which is a member state, is not. Moreover, in some cases, because of the migration crisis, Schengen has had to be abandoned, at least temporarily. The pressure from the Middle East is, of course, likely to continue and could affect Scotland if, after independence, it subscribed to the Schengen Agreement.

The Scottish government is keenly aware of the need for inward migration, because of the increasing number of dependents in its population, and has said it wants a different policy from England. Immigration, so far, has aroused less opposition in Scotland than in England but that may be partly because Scotland has had far fewer immigrants. It is likely that an independent Scotland would also want, like the Republic of Ireland, to remain in the UK's common travel area. This does not necessarily mean there could be no differences in immigration policy, but it would mean that Schengen, for Scotland, would not be compatible with the common travel area of the UK and Ireland. If Scotland was a full member state of the EU, it would be expected to accept membership of the Schengen Area as part of the *acquis communautaire*, unless, like Ireland, it obtained an opt-out. That may not be difficult but, if Scotland applied for membership not of the EU but of the EEA, it would probably not even be necessary, despite the fact other EEA members are also members of the Schengen Area.

Undoubtedly the EU's policy on inward migration is still without satisfactory agreement. Greece, one of the poorer member states and with its own serious problems, and Italy have borne the brunt of the inflow of refugees and it is unreasonable to expect them to cope with this without help. But that requires some difficult decisions to be taken and agreed and there is no sign yet of the issue being satisfactorily resolved.

The Euro

If Scotland was a member of the EU, it might be expected to express an intention to adopt the euro, since that is part of the *acquis communautaire*. But, as explained in Chapter 2, it could not be compelled to do so and, at present, it would not qualify as it does not meet one of the main qualifying criteria – a budget deficit below 3 per cent of GDP. If it was a member of the EEA rather than the EU, there would be no requirement to adopt the euro, although it could probably do so if it so wished, if and when it satisfied the criteria. The euro was introduced as the single currency partly because of the drive for increased integration generally but also because it was thought desirable, if not essential, to complete the single market. Member countries, it was argued, could not be expected to remove all forms of protection if some of them repeatedly had recourse of devaluation to make their economies more competitive against businesses in other member states.

Experience of the situation before the introduction of the euro was certainly not satisfactory. There were repeated devaluations and exchange rates between the different currencies did not always reflect the true economic strength of member states. Because of speculation or sometimes even government policy, they often tended to depart, even for long periods, from what could be regarded as realistic values. As early as 1987, the Padoa-Schioppa Committee for the European Commission pointed out that the Exchange Rate Mechanism (the ERM that preceded the euro) was unlikely to survive the liberalisation of capital movements.[3] The position was described by the committee as attempting co-existence with the 'inconsistent quartet': free trade; full capital mobility; fixed or managed exchange rates; and national autonomy in monetary policy. It was not surprising that, in these circumstances, there were complaints between member states about unfair competition and doubts about the ultimate survival of the single market.

By introducing the euro, however, the EU has not got rid of many of the pressures that caused the previous national currencies to have to change in value. It was not only speculation that caused previous fluctuations – often changes were needed to maintain the competitive position of member states' economies. And, if such an important tool for economic adjustment is removed, countries that become uncompetitive can suffer severe economic distress. This was particularly evident in Greece but has also resulted in extremely poor rates of economic growth in Italy. Spain and Portugal have also suffered. In Spain, unemployment rose to over 20 per cent and the *Indignados* movement resulted in huge demonstrations in 2011 and 2012 in all the major cities. Ireland suffered extreme distress during the euro crisis, when draconian austerity, far more severe than was suffered in Britain, was forced on it. Unemployment rose from under 5 per cent in the early 2000s to 7.3 per cent in 2012 and would have been much higher but for emigration. Government debt rose to 119 per cent of GDP. But, thankfully, Ireland has managed to recover and is now back to a satisfactory rate of growth with government debt back down to 59 per cent of GDP in 2019 and unemployment at 5 per cent.

There would have been serious difficulties in any event following the world banking crisis of 2009. But the eurozone crisis that followed was at least partly because the move to the single currency was incomplete and several of the countries that joined were not ready or properly prepared. In an important book that deals in detail with the problems of the European monetary union, Joseph Stiglitz, a former chairman of the US President's Council of Economic Advisers, a former Chief Economist at the World Bank and a Nobel Prize winner in Economics, shows the flaws in the European monetary union and the action that would be needed.[4] In federal countries, monetary union works because there is at least some mutualised debt, with responsibility shared by member states. There is also a bank deposit guarantee throughout the federation and usually the federal government is responsible for a large part of public expenditure on such matters as welfare and unemployment insurance. These things help to protect a member of the currency union if it is in difficulty following the collapse of a major industry or for some other reason. But the member states of the eurozone have none of these protections.

In the United States, Alexander Hamilton, the first Treasury Secretary, introduced federal debt, a mutualised debt for all the member states. This meant that the debt of one state was as secure as that of others so that there were no huge differences in interest rates. In the eurozone, this was fiercely resisted by Germany on the grounds that it was not a transfer union, since this would automatically have meant that some member states were carrying the deficits of others. In effect, this is what was seen as a 'free-rider' problem. But that is what happens in a monetary union and is illustrated in the UK by the fact that, as seen in Chapter 3, Scotland, Wales and Northern Ireland and all the regions of England are in budget deficit, apart from London, the South-East and the Eastern Region, which are in surplus. If there was no mutualised debt, with each region having its own budget and being responsible for its own debt, there would be differences in interest rates, depending on how the market judged their prospects of avoiding a default.

In the long run, therefore, if repeated crises are to be avoided, the eurozone is going to require what has been described as 'more Europe' – a banking union, a euro-wide guarantee of bank deposits and the mutualisation of the public debt of members. Without this, member states in difficulty face the prospect of high interest rates and the threat of insolvency, which can plunge them into a vicious downward spiral of ever-increasing difficulty. If these things are unacceptable because of fear that some states will become free riders, it means that the union is too large and that some members are not ready for it.

Furthermore, it was the sharing of taxation and public expenditure between the different levels of government, with, typically, at least 20 per cent the responsibility of central government and the remainder for the member states, that led the British economist Sir Donald MacDougall to conclude in a seminal report for the then EEC, as long ago as 1977, that much greater provision for fiscal transfers was essential before embarking on monetary union.[5]

Within most federal countries, there is an implicit commitment to equalisation between members to ensure the cohesion of integration. This can either take the form of richer states making up for the lower income of poorer states with transfers or a commitment to base public expenditure on need rather than what an individual state can afford. Within a centralised country such as the UK, this happens automatically. Indeed, it is only recently that much attention has been given to what fiscal transfers might be between the four nations and the English regions and, for the most part, the public are still unaware of them. There is no such 'fiscal federalism' in the EU and, although the structural funds and the cohesion fund are intended to help poorer areas, the European budget is still only around 1 per cent of the EU's GDP compared with about 20 per cent for central government in a typical federal state.

If the economy of the EU is really to become more integrated and cohesive, these are matters that need to be considered. Fiscal transfers are resisted by Germany and, especially, the German electorate which does not feel it has any responsibility to support the poorer members in this way. But, if European monetary union is to work, some such transfers will be necessary, just as they are in the successful monetary unions of the United States, Canada and Germany itself. In time, they would, of course, improve the economic performance of the whole union.

For a monetary union to be stable and work successfully, the member states also have to be able to keep their rates of inflation broadly in line with each other. Otherwise some members will become uncompetitive and suffer unemployment, while others will have export surpluses. This is what has happened in the EU and it is understandable that, if this is the result of poor economic policy, the member states in surplus will not want to carry the resulting debt of other members. Adoption of the single currency and a single interest rate meant that interest rates fell sharply in some member states, leading to an inflationary boom. Spain and Ireland both had a construction boom that was out of control. Greece had a spending spree.

The result was the eurozone crisis, which was particularly severe in Greece. Greece, in my view, which I think was widely shared, should never have joined the euro. In a study that I undertook for the Bank of Scotland in 1997, I thought that the adoption of the euro should have been limited to a small group of countries that could show that they had been able to keep their previous exchange rates stable and inflation rates similar to each other, thus remaining competitive without resorting to devaluation.[6] But the EU wanted as many members to join as possible. For Greece, it was obviously a mistake and it resulted in the country having to endure extreme hardship and a catastrophic fall in national output, worse than the 1930s' depression. The conversion of member states' debt to euros, with much of it funded by banks across the EU, meant that much of the money spent helping Greece went to pay off the loans of European banks. I thought that the EU should have spent its money helping Greece to leave the euro and reintroduce the drachma but it would have devalued sharply and the debt being in euros would have been an even greater burden and probably required the country to default. Clearly this was a disaster. The problems with the euro, however, have also led to very slow economic growth in Italy and much discontent there as well as in Spain, Portugal and Ireland.

Joe Stiglitz in his book casts considerable doubt on the EU's ability to resolve this without major changes in its policy.[7] The danger is that the EU will be unable to achieve its growth potential and will stagger on with high unemployment and periodic resort to austerity. He takes the view that it either has to have more of the features of a federal state described above or it must free some of the countries from the constraints of monetary union. If it was not for the monetary union, Germany's currency would have risen substantially, reducing its balance of payments surplus and the currency of several southern European countries would have fallen in value, so reducing their deficits. One possibility would be to have a 'northern euro' and a 'southern euro' at least until more of the features of a federal state with EU-wide bank deposit guarantees, mutualisation of debt and some centralisation of welfare expenditure, for example on unemployment, can be introduced. Some people have hailed the EU's decision to provide a fund of some 750 billion euros to help recovery from the COVID crisis as a first step in moving towards this.

From Scotland's point of view in wanting to rejoin the single market, if not full membership of the EU, the prosperity of Europe matters as it will affect Scottish EU trade. If, as an independent state, it were to join the EU, it would seem most unwise to join the eurozone in the present circumstances, even if it met the criteria for doing so. It would lose the ability to adjust its exchange rate and interest rates, two of the main tools available for economic management. If it becomes a member of the EEA, these tools would still be available should circumstances require it.

The problems of managing the enlarged EU, the difficulties over migration and, above all, continuing doubts over the euro show that there is much uncertainty at present over the European project. But the leaders of most member states are still heavily committed to it and, whatever happens, they recognise it is important that the EU continues as a single market. While Scotland's trade with the EU will be affected by whatever measures affect the latter's prosperity, the EU with its population of 440 million will still be Scotland's main overseas market. It would, therefore, still be extremely important for Scotland to seek membership of the single market through the EEA if not full membership of the EU, if it decides to become independent.

Finally, it is worth noting that the problems of the EU monetary union are not unique to it. If Scotland were to become independent and either seek to retain monetary union with the UK or simply use the UK currency on a 'sterlingisation' basis, it would presumably lose the UK-wide bank deposit guarantee and the mutualisation of debt as well as the support it presently gets financially through the sharing of public expenditure costs with the UK exchequer. That suggests that such a monetary arrangement would run into trouble sooner or later causing serious problems for the independent country.

Summary and conclusion

Should there be a referendum?

When I started to write this, polls were suggesting that support for independence in Scotland was continuing to rise, with one poll showing 58 per cent in favour – a bigger margin than the 2016 Brexit referendum achieved for Leave in the UK. That is not so clear now, with polls showing approximately a 50–50 split between those favouring independence and those not wanting any change. They will probably continue to be volatile. It seems that the decline may be partly a result of problems within the SNP. But it may also be that, as people think more about the momentous change that independence would mean, they become more hesitant in backing it. The result of the May 2021 Scottish election showed a strengthened vote and a majority for the two parties in favour of independence, although it fell one seat short of an overall majority for the SNP on its own. The pressure for an independence referendum therefore remains strong.

The Prime Minister, Boris Johnson, has said that there will not be such a referendum in the lifetime of the present UK Parliament and that the 2014 referendum was said, even by SNP leaders, to be a once in a generation event. That is simply not credible not least because, following the EU referendum, which has resulted in the UK leaving the EU, subsequent policies took no account of the result in Scotland, which had voted by a majority of 62 per cent to remain. Not a single Scottish local authority area voted in favour of Leave. It cannot of course be assumed that all those who voted to Remain in the EU would vote for Scottish independence once the full implications of that – such as a border with the rest of the UK, the financial implications for tax and public expenditure and probably a new currency – become clear. A referendum would certainly be divisive but to try to refuse a referendum would not be democratically credible and, in my view, eventually risk some potentially dangerous extra-parliamentary action from elements in the independence movement.

It would clearly not be sensible to have a referendum while the consequences of the COVID pandemic are still being dealt with, and that means it should not be in 2022. The First Minister has said that she would want it during the lifetime of the new Scottish Parliament and the suggestion has been made that this might mean sometime in 2023. All the forecasts suggest that leaving the EU is expected to do serious damage to the Scottish economy. Despite the last-minute agreement on trade with the EU of Christmas 2020, ending Scotland's membership of the EU single market will still do both short-term and long-term damage. Some businesses may leave Scotland, while others may decide to invest elsewhere in Europe rather than in Scotland, hitting the inward investment on which Scotland has relied. On the other hand, if independence means that Scotland would face a hard border for its trade with the rest of the UK, which is significantly greater than its trade with the EU, that could be even more damaging.

After the experience of recent referenda both in Scotland and the UK, it would not be acceptable to require some kind of super majority in the referendum result, as is sometimes suggested. Previous referenda, of which there have now been several, have set the precedent as all of them, apart from the Scottish devolution referendum of 1979, were determined by a straight majority. This includes the referendum in 2016 on leaving the EU, where the majority had a very narrow margin. The Cunningham amendment to the 1979 Scottish devolution referendum Bill, which required a majority amounting to at least 40 per cent of the whole registered Scottish electorate, was greatly resented.

For any referendum, there is an onus on those who favour independence to set out their reasons in clear and fair terms why people should vote for it but it is also up to those who favour the status quo to set out their case fully and argue it so that the electorate are properly informed before they vote. There can be a danger that voters who feel disaffected with the status quo will vote for change without understanding its full implications. That may well have been the case for many with the EU referendum.

If the Scottish referendum result was in favour of independence, there could, therefore, as Sir John Major has suggested, be a case for a confirmatory vote once the terms negotiated became clear. The case for this would be particularly strong if the vote was close. Recent polls suggest that, if such a confirmatory vote had been held, the 2016 EU referendum result might have been overturned when the full implications of what it involved were understood.

One cannot expect the public to fully understand all the issues until they are properly explored. How many people in Scotland realise that independence would mean a hard border with England with customs and probably passport control, unless Scotland decided to stay in the UK single market and accept UK rules on trade and migration?

Should there be an alternative of beefed-up devolution or proper federalism? Gordon Brown has argued for this and it may become official Labour Party policy, having been taken up by Keir Starmer, the party leader. He has said there should be a constitutional commission and appears to be considering major constitutional reform in the UK, possibly with a federal structure giving power to the English regions as well as Scotland, Wales and Northern Ireland. There might also be reform replacing the House of Lords with a chamber in which there would be regional representation. All of this is badly needed and long overdue but there is no support for it in the Conservative Party and, even if Labour came to power in the next UK election, it would take a long time for such a major change to be agreed and implemented. It must be doubtful if public opinion in Scotland would be prepared to wait that long when the independence lobby is so strong.

If there is a Referendum, what kind of Independence?

At this stage, one cannot make an assumption on what the result of a referendum would be as there is much to be explored, explained to the public and debated. But, if a referendum were to lead to a vote for independence, what sort of independence should it be? Independence while remaining in the UK single market, with sterling used as the currency on a sterlingisation basis, would not be satisfactory. There would be no sharing of public expenditure costs, no fund for equalising expenditure on needs and no Scottish control of the currency, the exchange rate or of interest rates – some of the main levers for economic management – and this would put Scotland in the position of being in a monetary union without the means to make it work satisfactorily.

Other options are reapplying for membership of the EU, which would probably take some years to be accepted, with a possible veto from any member state concerned about secessionist tendencies in its own country, or membership of EFTA and the EEA. Full EU membership and membership of the EEA would both give membership of the EU single market. The former would require Scotland to have a hard border with the rest of the UK, just like any other EU member state. EEA membership would give Scotland membership of the EU single market but not the EU Customs Union. While also involving a border with controls and checks, it would, therefore, enable it to negotiate its own trading arrangements with the rest of the UK and other non-EU countries. Any imported goods from the rest of the UK would have to have certificates of origin if re-exported from Scotland to the EU. This would be bureaucratic and cumbersome, imposing delays that do not presently exist. That would undoubtedly be unpopular and cause difficulties, given the heavy dependence Scotland presently has on trade with other parts of the UK. It would require major adjustments but it should be manageable, as it is with other EEA members. The common agriculture and fisheries policies would not apply and the single market would, therefore, not cover agricultural and fisheries products on which there would have to be negotiation. But there would be no expectation for Scotland to join the eurozone. Membership would be a two-stage process – Scotland would first be required to join EFTA and then, once accepted as a member, apply to join the EEA. Agreement for Scotland to join the EEA would be required from the three EFTA states that are members and also the 27 EU members. While unexpected problems cannot be excluded, it is likely that membership of EFTA and the EEA could be agreed more quickly than full membership of the EU.

My view is, therefore, that, if Scotland was to choose in a referendum to become independent, membership of EFTA and of the EEA would be more appropriate, at least initially, than full membership of the EU. This would give Scotland membership of the EU single market, which was what the Scottish government wanted in its 2016 paper, and it should be less damaging to its trade with the rest of the UK than full membership of the EU.[1] Membership of the EEA, however, would not give Scotland membership of the European Council or Parliament and it would not have a European Commissioner.

Even with Boris Johnson's Christmas agreement on free trade with the EU, there is no acceptance of EU regulations and the agreement does not apply to services. Both of these would adversely affect Scotland's trade with Europe, if it remained part of the UK. If Scotland becomes a member state, therefore, either of the EU or the EEA, the share of trade with Europe would probably grow more rapidly. Already, over the last few years, Scottish trade with the EU has grown faster than trade with the rest of the UK or the rest of the world. Scotland would have the benefit of trading with the largest trading block in the world and also share in all the trading relationships the EU has negotiated with other countries.

Difficulties that an Independent Scotland would Face

An independent Scotland would inevitably face some serious difficulties, however. In 2019–20, there was a budget deficit of well over 8 per cent of GDP, according to the Scottish government's own publication, and, in 2020–21, it was substantially higher at 22.4 per cent, as a result of the COVID pandemic. Clearly, this would be unsustainable. Scotland is far from being alone in this – Wales, Northern Ireland and all the English regions, apart from London, the South-East and the Eastern Region, would have budget deficits and, on a per-head basis, Scotland's deficit would be lower than many others. The deficit can be expected to reduce when the economy gets back to normal but it has risen more proportionally than the UK deficit and it is not clear if it will get back to pre-COVID levels. As an independent state, the Scottish budget deficit would have to be dealt with without any funds being transferred from the rest of the UK. This would be a major challenge, analogous to the situation in which some of the EU member states found themselves in the eurozone after the financial crisis. Unless steps could be taken to enable the economy to grow considerably so that tax income increased, there would have to be tax rises and cuts to public expenditure. There could, therefore, be the prospect of austerity lasting several years.

The UK government's debt is meanwhile, as a consequence of COVID, now over 100 per cent of GDP. It will be a considerable time before this settles and it becomes clear how the UK proposes to deal with it after the pandemic has passed. But, in time, an independent Scotland would not only have to eliminate its budget deficit but also agree to take a share of the accumulated debt.

Quantitative easing by the Bank of England, however, has resulted in about a third of the debt being held by the central bank, on which it returns the interest due to the government. This would be something to be settled in negotiation, either excluding it from Scotland's share or agreeing to transfer it to a new Scottish central bank. If the Scottish government takes responsibility for paying a share of the debt, it follows that it should also receive a share of the assets, including the foreign exchange reserves.

The analysis based on the Scottish government's input–output tables shows that there would be a substantial deficit on the current account of the balance of foreign payments. Scotland's exports overseas exceed imports but imports from the rest of the UK substantially exceed exports. An independent Scotland could not expect large inflows of capital to cover this deficit, now that North Sea oil is well past its peak, so the resulting balance of payments deficit would not be sustainable. Trying to make the Scottish economy more competitive by forcing down labour costs, as has happened with some countries in the eurozone, would be extremely painful and would take a long time. Furthermore, getting an increase in investment in such circumstances to improve the country's competitive position would be difficult.

The case for a Scottish Currency

This suggests there is a need for Scotland to have its own currency. And the new currency should be allowed to settle at a level that would make the economy competitive, thereby boosting exports, stimulating the economy and improving both the budget balance and the balance of payments. It is possible that a separate currency for Scotland might be forced by market pressure, as it was for Slovakia when it separated from the Czech Republic. If this happened – or if it was recognised that a new Scottish currency was in prospect – the associated uncertainty would be very bad for business. Probably the currency would settle at a level that involved devaluation. This could result in a need to control any resulting inflation and could impact on living standards, until the benefits of devaluation resulted in improved growth. Introducing a new Scottish currency would, therefore, be far from simple and some of the financial institutions in Scotland that have the bulk of their customers in England might choose to relocate. But, in the end, if well handled, it could improve the performance and longer-term prospects for Scotland.

Other demands on the Scottish Budget

An independent Scotland would also find that there were many other demands on its tax revenue. Healthcare has been seriously underfunded in the UK for many years, as the COVID pandemic has demonstrated. The funding of care and care homes is also inadequate and needs major reform, as the Feeley Report proposes. Inevitably this will require significantly increased expenditure. Education, likewise, will be a major claim on the budget. The performance of pupils in many schools is disappointing, especially in deprived areas – with statistics showing some pupils ending up lacking sufficient skills in literacy and numeracy to enable them to get worthwhile jobs. There has been much criticism of the handling of school education by the Scottish government and a major change now seems necessary. Universities have been very hard hit by the epidemic. In addition, their dependence on the fees of foreign students has meant there had to be a cap on the number of Scottish students admitted. This is certainly unsatisfactory. The whole system of university fees needs to be reviewed but, whatever the outcome, it can be expected to be an additional charge on the government's budget.

Vocational skills have long been given insufficient priority in the UK, in comparison with university degrees. In Scotland, there have been amalgamations, reducing the number of colleges of further education. It is important that vocational skills should be properly valued and not treated as less important than university qualifications. There has been a shortage of many types of skilled worker, as the large number who came from eastern EU countries to find jobs here demonstrated, many of whom have played a valuable part in the economy.

The largest category of public expenditure, as in the whole UK, however, is social protection. In 2019–20, this comprised 30 per cent of all public expenditure in Scotland – more than health and education combined. At present, 75 per cent of this is funded by the UK government but, if Scotland was to become independent, it would be responsible for the full cost and there would be demands to increase both eligibility and payments. Just under half of the total is spent on the state pension but the other items are more variable, depending on the state of the economy and, in particular, on the level of unemployment. A significant amount of Universal Credit goes on supporting those in work, whose pay is inadequate or those who can only find part-time work. This means that, in such cases, the state is supporting employers who do not or cannot pay their employees adequately. While unemployment, thankfully, has been low, there are too many people in poorly paid or unsatisfactory jobs with little or no security. Raising the minimum wage might just mean that these jobs are lost altogether. But the aim must be to have an economy where there is sufficient prosperity for this to be unnecessary. It is part of the inequality that has been a feature of the UK economy but it would be hard to rectify and, in the meantime, there would be demands both to increase Universal Credit and to abolish the long delay that applicants face in receiving it.

Management of the Economy

If any of the above demands on public expenditure are to be met, raising some taxes could help but would be counterproductive if it resulted in businesses or individuals choosing to move their location south of the border. There is, therefore, a need to increase the economy's growth. Scotland has the institutions needed to encourage growth. Grants and loans are available and the enterprise agencies have powers to assist. Much will be needed to repair the damage caused to the economy by the COVID pandemic and the report by the committee chaired by Benny Higgins makes valuable recommendations.[2] Clearly, much is hoped for from the new Scottish National Investment Bank (SNIB). It is to focus on helping firms achieve innovative growth, to invest in infrastructure and to help finance opportunities arising from action to stave off climate change. But it should also prioritise encouraging more growth from start-ups and scale-ups in small and medium-sized firms where, despite much attention from the enterprise agencies, there is still a need for more to be achieved. It should also provide 'patient capital' for the many companies that have good long-term prospects but have struggled as a result of the pandemic and been forced to borrow to make up for loss of income. It is important that such companies are not lost to the economy or are prevented from investing because of the overhang of debt. Some would be in danger, if they survive, of becoming 'zombie' companies because they would feel unable to finance investment. The SNIB could fill an important role by providing equity or loans to keep such companies alive and able to invest.

Despite its many papers on the economy and the low level of unemployment in Scotland before the pandemic, the Scottish government does not have a good record in its management of the industrial economy. It has several major problematic investments. Much has been said about the opportunities from onshore and offshore wind and Burntisland

Fabrications (BiFab) was one of the main companies making structures for this market. The collapse of BiFab, in which the government had a substantial stake, was, therefore, serious. It will not do to blame the company's collapse on the Canadian owners, EU competition rules or subsidised competition. No doubt there were problems from all of these but one cannot imagine any other country, either inside or outside the EU, allowing what was expected to be a major opportunity for the economy to end up so disastrously. The announcement in February 2021 that InfraStrata had taken over the BiFab yards at Methil in Fife and Arnish in Lewis, which are to trade under the name of Harland and Wolff together with its shipyards in Belfast and Devon, is very welcome. It is to be hoped that this will now secure a good future for these two yards but it will have cost the Scottish government dearly for its earlier support and a loss on its purchase of a shareholding in the business.

The government has nationalised Prestwick Airport and, therefore, has responsibility for its future and continuing costs. There needs to be a proper appraisal of whether the airport actually has a future in the light of the major investment over several years that has taken place at both Abbotsinch and Turnhouse, since both of these airports can now take the long-haul traffic that previously had to use Prestwick. Unpopular though closure would certainly be, especially in Ayrshire, it makes no sense to keep the airport going with all the cost that implies, if there is insufficient demand to make it profitable.

There is also the major problem of the two ferries to serve the Scottish islands being built for CalMac at Fergusons ship-yard in Port Glasgow. These are now expected to cost twice as much as the original contract and are already many years late. Obviously there was something seriously amiss with the negotiated contract. But, whatever the reasons, the decision to nationalise the yard simply transferred the responsibility to government. Jim McColl, whose company owned Fergusons, having rescued it from its previous time in administration, did not seem to think nationalisation was the solution and he may be right.

As this was being written, a further problem with serious potential liability for the Scottish government arose from the collapse of Greensill Capital. This company had financed Sanjeev Gupta's GFG Alliance and the latter could, as a result of its loans being called in, be forced into insolvency. Through its subsidiary, Liberty Steel, GFG Alliance had taken owner-ship of the two remaining Scottish steel mills, Dalzell and Clydebridge, and through another subsidiary, Alvance, had taken over the aluminium smelter and associated hydro plant at Fort William. The Scottish government had given a 25-year guarantee on the supply of electricity from the hydro plant. The solving of this problem is primarily for the UK govern-ment, as GFG Alliance through Liberty Steel has substantial ownership of steel plants in England. But, if the company fails, not only will there be serious consequences resulting in unem-ployment but the Scottish government could also face the cost of its guarantee on the hydroelectricity at Fort William.

There was clearly a need for someone with experience of sorting out industry in difficulty to take a firm grip of all of these problems. One has the impression that nationalisation or, in the case of BiFab, taking a major stake in the company, was resorted to without a clear plan for the recovery and future of these companies. If the Scottish National Investment Bank is expected now to take over the government's shareholding in these companies, it is important that it has the expertise to tackle such problems rather than simply acting as a holding company.

Energy and North Sea Oil

North Sea oil is now past its peak and, unless there is an unex-pected rise in oil prices, the value of the revenues will remain much more modest than at the time of the last referendum.

Because of climate change, there is also strong pressure to move away from fossil fuels. So North Sea oil can no longer be looked to as the solution to any financial problems Scotland has to face. There is, however, remarkable developments in forms of green energy, with wind now supplying a large part of Scotland's electricity needs. It is not clear whether this will be sufficient when the two nuclear stations have to close and there is clearly a need for a plan to deal with this situation. The problem with wind energy is that, apart from its environmental impact, it cannot always be relied on because the wind is not constant. Similar problems apply to solar power. Further development of pumped-storage hydro to even out the supply could offer part of a solution but the most promising prospect would appear to be in the development of hydrogen, which could be manufactured during times when electricity supply is plentiful and be available when needed. Blue hydrogen might replace much of the natural gas supply and green hydrogen could be available for other uses, but that would require a significant increase in electricity for its production.

The Financial Sector

The financial sector is of major importance to the Scottish economy, employing around over 100,000 people if the indirect effects are included. It would obviously be affected by Scotland becoming independent – unfavourably, if financial companies that had the bulk of their customers in other parts of the UK felt a need to move out of Scotland but favourably, if being once again in the EU single market with 'passporting' rights gave them opportunities they had previously enjoyed and that Brexit was denying them. The relocation of financial businesses to Dublin and to the Continent suggests that this effect could be quite significant. It is not possible to judge which of these effects would be more significant and Scotland would be unlikely to be able to offer the very low corporation tax that is one of the attractions that Dublin offers.

Mortgages and Pensions

As an independent state, rates of interest in Scotland would probably be somewhat higher than in the UK. This is partly a matter of scale. The Scottish financial market would be smaller and it would also be new. The UK has never, since the foundation of the Bank of England in the seventeenth century, defaulted on its debt. Scotland would be able to rely on no such record and it would take time for a sound reputation in managing debt to be acquired. The rate of interest on mortgages would therefore reflect this.

Both mortgages and pensions would be affected by the introduction of a Scottish currency. To avoid exchange risk, mortgages would have to be taken out afresh in the new currency. State pensions and public pensions would automatically be changed to the Scottish currency but private pensions would be paid by the providers as they are now with the recipients either gaining or losing from exchange movements, unless they were rearranged in the Scottish currency. A substantial amount of the private pensions would be cross border which is unusual in the EU and, under the rules, would have to be fully funded. This could be a problem although the IORP II Directive gives greater flexibility in meeting this requirement.

Government action has, in the past, affected both state pensions and private pensions. Pressures on the public finances could affect the state pension although, before the 2014 referendum, the Scottish government gave assurances that it would be protected. Private pensions, unless provided by a Scottish financial company, could continue to be affected by any action the UK government might take, just as has happened in the past.

The European Union and its Problems

The expectation is that the government of an independent Scotland would apply to rejoin the EU, although the analysis in this book suggests that it would be more appropriate and easier to seek membership of the EEA. The EU undoubtedly has its problems, as Chapter 10 has shown. Enlargement to 27 members has made it more difficult to agree on policy issues. Despite trying, there has been no agreement on handling the large flow of immigrants from war in the Middle East or from Africa. And, despite the willingness of Germany to take a large share, other countries have resisted agreement, with the result that countries in the south of Europe, notably Greece and Italy, have not had the help they needed.

More serious, however, for Europe's prosperity has been the continuing imbalance in the eurozone countries. Germany, the strongest economy, has had very low inflation and ended up with a large balance of payments surplus. Other countries, notably in the south of Europe, have become less competitive with resulting deficits and all the pressure has been on them, rather than countries in surplus, to reduce this imbalance. The problem is that the monetary union is incomplete. It needs a banking union, with Europe-wide deposit guarantees, mutualisation of much of the debt and the eurozone countries collectively taking responsibility for funding a significant share of public expenditure as is normal in federal countries.

To rest on the German view that the EU is not a transfer union is not tenable if the eurozone is to prosper and avoid future crises. The only satisfactory alternatives would be either for Germany to leave the eurozone, allow its exchange rate to rise and the currency of others still using the euro to fall or to devise a scheme, as Joseph Stiglitz suggests, of having a northern and southern euro, until the monetary union can be made more complete. It seems unlikely that either of these courses will be adopted and that the eurozone will be left to muddle along without the problem being tackled. This will have a damaging effect on growth, especially in the deficit countries until, eventually, there is another crisis and one or more of the members decide they have to leave the euro.

Despite this depressing outlook, it still makes sense for Scotland, if it becomes independent, to foster its trading links with the EU. It will still be Scotland's largest overseas market and the largest trading block in the world. But the problems of the eurozone provide an illustration, if one were needed, of the difficulties that can arise with an incomplete monetary union. An independent Scotland should, therefore, not join the euro and, although it would be sensible to peg its currency either to the euro or the pound, after it has found a level that makes the economy competitive, it should maintain the ability to adjust its exchange rate if that is needed to ensure the continued prosperity of the economy.

Conclusion

Much has been written about Scottish independence in recent years. Usually, this has focussed on the development of political thought that underlies the growth in the nationalist movement or, on the other hand, emphasises a strong remaining loyalty to the UK. It is certainly the case, however, that there is a feeling of democratic deficiency when Scotland's votes are so much at variance with the majority that is elected at Westminster, as is the situation presently with a strong Brexiteer element in the UK governing party. The Conservative Party, which was a major force in Scotland in the 1950s, has not fully recovered in Scotland from the Thatcher years, after which, in the 1997 election, it lost all its Scottish seats in the UK Parliament. Although it is now the main opposition in the Scottish Parliament, it is a long way from catching up the SNP. The Labour Party, which dominated Scotland during and after the Thatcher years and formed a coalition government with the Liberal Democrats in the first years of devolution, is still also a shadow of its former self. If Scotland continues to vote for a party that is not in government at Westminster, as it did so clearly by voting for Labour in the 1980s and early 90s and again recently with the SNP, it is bound to feel, in some respect, disenfranchised. This, it seems to me, is the essence of the present discontent and it is a situation that now seems very unlikely to change.

In this short book, I have tried to explain the economic issues – both for and against – that independence would present. What are Scotland's future prospects? Brexit has altered them significantly. The choice Scotland will have to make is not easy. It could keep the status quo as part of the UK, maintain its position in the UK single market and keep the pound as its currency. It would then simply have to cope with the damage to trade and investment that Brexit is likely to cause. The damage over the longer term may be the greatest problem because of the effect on international companies that might have considered investment in Scotland. I would hope that there would still be fiscal transfers from the UK to help with public expenditure.

Alternatively, if the people of Scotland vote for independence in a referendum, it could aim to join the EEA, restoring its membership of the EU single market and get the best arrangements it can on trade with the rest of the UK. But that would undoubtedly mean, even with a successful negotiation, a border with customs posts at Gretna, Berwick and Carter Bar and probably a new Scottish currency. Even with a free-trade arrangement with the rest of the UK, there would inevitably be bureaucracy and disruption to Scottish–UK trade, Scotland's largest market. It would also have to cope with the fiscal deficit.

Membership of the EU single market could restore Scotland's trade with Europe, her largest overseas market, and might perhaps result in more companies choosing to locate and invest in Scotland to do business with Europe. This effect might be substantial but, at this stage, it is impossible to say and the border with the rest of the UK might result in others moving to another part of the UK if that was where they had their main market.

It is far from clear, at this stage, whether the Scottish public is prepared for the imposition of a border with England and the rest of the UK, for measures to tackle the fiscal deficit or for the introduction of a new currency. The upheaval caused by leaving the UK would undoubtedly be major and costly – it might well result in a fall in living standards for several years and significant inflation. It is not clear that this is understood even by those who seek independence.

It is perhaps in the end a difficult choice between the short and the long term. In the long run, Scotland could perhaps do better economically as an independent state linked with the EU and its huge market than continuing as part of the UK but that could certainly not be guaranteed and would depend on the wisdom or otherwise of the policies of future Scottish governments.

Scotland might hope to emulate the success of the Republic of Ireland, which now has a national income per head above that of the UK, despite it having been not much more than 50 per cent of the UK average when it became independent in 1922. But it should be remembered that Ireland did very poorly economically for the first 30 years or so of its independence until the late 1950s when policies began to be followed that produced strong economic growth. Even now, however, Ireland has remained a low public expenditure country and has not followed the high public expenditure and high taxation model of Scandinavia, which many in Scotland apparently see as their goal.

The more the adverse effects of Brexit become apparent, the more support for independence may rise – especially if the UK government fails to work effectively with the devolved government of Scotland. But the more Scottish people become aware of the scale of the huge upheaval and uncertainty that independence would cause – the difficulty of eliminating the budgetary deficit and restructuring the economy in favour of manufactured exports, the imposition of a border with the rest of the UK for trade and migration and a new currency – the more people might have second thoughts and vote for the status quo. My purpose, in this book, was to explain these economic issues and I have attempted to do so impartially.

I have not tried to tackle issues other than those that affect the economy. In particular, there are serious and major implications for defence and security. These, although not covered here, need to be considered, along with cultural and other issues. There would also be implications for families that would have members on both sides of the border and it needs to be recognised that many people have a loyalty to the country that the UK has been for over 300 years. These are all considerations that would have a major effect on the result of a referendum.

Notes

Introduction

1 The growth of the SNP and the philosophy behind it is fully explained in Professor Ben Jackson's book *The Case for Scottish Independence*, Cambridge University Press, 2020.

Chapter 1

1 Michael Gove has spoken of the importance of a 'settled will' before agreeing to a referendum. This phrase was originally used in relation to devolution in Scotland.
2 'Scotland's Place in Europe', Scottish Government, Edinburgh, 2016.
3 Sir John Major, a speech delivered to the Middle Temple and reported in *The Times*, 10 November 2010.
4 See two articles in *Byline Times* by James Melville and Hardeep Matharu, 21 and 27 January 2020.
5 J D Gallagher, 'Progressive Federalism: a different way of looking at the United Kingdom', Fabian Society, 2019, and Andrew Blick, 'Federalism: The UK's Future?', the Federal Trust, 2016.
6 Ben Thomson, *Scottish Home Rule*, Birlinn, 2020.

Chapter 2

1 *Britain's Decision*, Charlie Jeffrey and Ray Perman (eds), p. 29, Chapter 3, David Bell, The David Hume Institute, Centre on Constitutional Change, Hunter Foundation, June 2016.

2 Article 9 of the EEA Treaty. I am indebted to Professor Christophe Hillion for this.

3 'Scotland's Place in Europe', Scottish Government, Edinburgh, 2016.

Chapter 3

1 'Scotland – the New Case for Optimism', report of the Sustainable Growth Commission, May 2018.

2 Ireland's GDP per head is some 20 per cent higher than GNP because there is a large payment of dividends and interest abroad on foreign investments, so GNP is the better measure for comparison. Most estimates of Irish GDP per head put it well above the UK level.

3 'Government and Revenue and Expenditure, Scotland, 2020–21', Scottish Government, August 2021.

4 See Gers, Covid and Scottish Independence (revisiting economic and fiscal arguments around a Second Independence Referendum), John McLaren, scottish-trends.co.uk, August 2020, for fuller analysis.

5 'Fair Shares for All', Final Report of the National Review of Resource Allocation for the NHS in Scotland, Scottish Executive Health Department, July 1999.

6 Increased greatly because of the pandemic.

7 Independent Commission on Funding and Finance for Wales, Cardiff, July 2010.

8 'Scotland's Future: Your Guide to an Independent Scotland, Scottish Government', 2013.

9 Stephanie Kelton, *The Deficit Myth*, John Murray, 2020.

10 'Scotland – the New Case for Optimism', report of the Sustainable Growth Commission, May 2018.

11 See my book *Scottish Independence: Weighing up the Economics*, Birlinn, 2014.

12 'The Scottish economy: seeking an advantage?', David Bell, in *Scotland's Economic Future*, Donald MacKay (ed.), Reform Scotland, 2010.

13 'Government Expenditure and Revenue Scotland 2019–20', Chapter 2, table 2.3.

14 Mervyn King, *The End of Alchemy – Money, Banking and the Future of the Global Economy*, Little Brown, 2016, pp 243–249.

15 'Professor Ronald MacDonald on GERS', www.scotland inunion.co.uk/post/professor-ronald-macdonald-on-gers

16 Jo Eric Murkens, with Peter Jones and Michael Keating, *Scottish Independence: a Practical Guide*, EUP, Edinburgh, 2002, Part 2, pp 143–4.

17 Joseph E. Stiglitz, *The Euro and its Threat to the Future of Europe*, Allen Lane, 2016. Stephanie Kelton, *The Deficit Myth*, John Murray, 2020.

Chapter 4

1 'Independent Review of Adult Social Care in Scotland', Scottish Government, February 202.

2 'The Thunderer' column in *The Times*, 20 November 2020.

3 *The Times*, 8 December 2020.

4 'A Teaching Profession for the 21st Century: the Report of the Committee of Inquiry into Professional Conditions of Service for Teachers'.

5 Alexander McCall Smith, 'What are our Universities For?', *The Scotsman*, 8 July 2020.

Chapter 5

1 See my *Scotland's Economic Progress 1951–1960*, George Allen and Unwin Ltd, London, 1965, p. 37.

2 'The Scottish economy: seeking an advantage?', David

Bell, in *Scotland's Economic Future*, Donald MacKay (ed.), Reform Scotland, 2010.

3   See Ray Perman, *Hubris: How HBOS Wrecked the Best Bank in Britain*, Birlinn Ltd, 2012.

Chapter 6

1   'Statistics of Government Revenues from UK Oil and Gas Production', HM Revenue & Customs, London, July 2020.

2   'Scotland's Future', Scottish Government, November 2013, and 'The Scottish Government's Oil and Gas Analytical Bulletin', March 2013.

Chapter 7

1   'Scotland's Energy Future', Royal Society of Edinburgh, June 2019.

2   'The Future of Energy in Scotland', Scottish Government, 2017.

3   'Energy Statistics for Scotland', Scottish Government, December 2020.

4   Gordon Hughes, 'The Performance of Wind Farms in the United Kingdom and Denmark', Renewable Energy Foundation, 2012.

5   Alistair Munro, 'Coire Glas hydro scheme approved by Scottish Government', *The Press and Journal*, 16 October 2020.

6   'Powering Fair Isle', Scottish Government, 12 October 2018.

7   'The Future of Energy in Scotland: Scottish Energy Strategy', Scottish Government, 2017.

8   'Scotland's Energy Future', Royal Society of Edinburgh, June 2019.

9   See Tom Russell, 'Port of Cromarty Firth unveils hydrogen hub plans', www.4coffshore.com, 5 March 2021.

Chapter 8

1 'Scotland analysis: Financial services and banking', UK Government, May 2013.

2 Jeremy Peat and Owen Kelly, 'Brexit and the Scottish Financial Services Sector', International Public Policy Institute, University of Strathclyde, October 2016.

3 Sarah Hall, 'What does the Brexit Trade Deal mean for Financial Services?', UK in a Changing Europe, 27 December 2020.

Chapter 9

1 Reported in the *Daily Telegraph*, 21 May 2013.

2 'Scotland's Pensions Future: What Pensions Arrangements Would Scotland Need?', ICAS, April 2013.

3 'Pensions in an Independent Scotland', Scottish Government, September 2013.

4 'Scottish Independence: The Implications for Pensions', NAPF, November 2013.

5 The RPI includes the cost of mortgage interest payments and council tax, which are not included in the CPI while some other items are. The result is that inflation, as measured by the two indices, differs from month to month with sometimes one and sometimes the other showing the greater increase.

6 HM Treasury, Budget, 2010.

7 'A New Pension Settlement for the Twenty-First Century', Second Report of the Commission, 2005, p 119.

8 'Scotland's Future: Your Guide to an Independent Scotland', Scottish Government, Edinburgh, November 2013, p. 146.

9 'Pensions in an Independent Scotland', Scottish Government, September 2013, also in 'Scotland's Future', November 2013.

10 'Independent Public Service Pensions Commission: Final Report by Lord Hutton', HM Treasury, March 2011.

11   Ibid., p. 55.

12   Alex Brummer, *The Great Pensions Robbery: How New Labour Betrayed Retirement*, Random House Business Books, 2010, p. 5.

13   *Pensions in an Independent Scotland*, Scottish Government, September 2013, p. 78.

14   'Scottish Independence: The Implications for Pensions', NAPF, November 2013, p. 11.

Chapter 10

1   In 2004, the Czech Republic, Estonia, Hungary, Latvia, Lithuania, Poland, Slovakia and Slovenia and, in 2007, Bulgaria and Romania.

2   Paolo Cecchini, 'Europe 1992: the Overall Challenge', SEC (88) 524, Brussels, April 1988.

3   Tommaso Padoa-Schioppa, 'Efficiency, Stability, and Equity', a report to the European Commission, Brussels, 1987.

4   Joseph E. Stiglitz, *The Euro and its Threat to the Future of Europe*, Allen Lane, 2016.

5   'Report of the Study Group on the Role of Public Finance in European Integration', (MacDougall Report), European Commission, Brussels, 1977.

6   Gavin McCrone, 'European Monetary Union and Regional Development', David Hume Papers, Vol.5 No.1, Spring 1997, Edinburgh University Press.

7   Joseph E. Stiglitz, *The Euro and its Threat to the Future of Europe*, Allen Lane, 2016

Chapter 11

1   'Scotland's Place in Europe', Scottish Government, Edinburgh, 2016.

2   'Towards a robust, resilient wellbeing economy for Scotland', Report of the Advisory Group on Economic Recovery, Scottish Government, 2020.

Index